Dead Man's H

A Thriller

Seymour Matthews

Samuel French - London
New York - Toronto - Hollywood

DEAD MAN'S HAND

First performed at the Frinton Theatre, Frinton, Essex, on 30th July 1984, with the following cast of characters:

Jennifer/Kate	Alison Temple Savage
Brian/Martin	Carl Carpenter
David/Derek	John D. Collins
Corinne/Angela	Jilly Bond
Franco	Giles Watling
Pamela	Angela Lavers

The play was directed by Seymour Matthews

The action of the play takes place in the lounge of an Italian villa

ACT I Scene 1 Dusk on a summer's evening
       Scene 2 Later the same evening

ACT II Scene 1 A moment later
       Scene 2 A moment later

Time—the present

ACT I

SCENE 1

The lounge of an Italian villa. Dusk on a summer's evening

The room is furnished with English antiques including a sofa, armchair, large table and a cocktail cabinet. In addition there is a side table complete with a table lamp. There are french windows C back leading on to a patio and a door on the R leading to the kitchen. On the L an archway leads to the hall, front door and the stairs

As the CURTAIN *rises the stage is dimly lit, the remains of daylight coming through the french windows*

We hear the sound of a car departing, then Jennifer enters from the hall and looks for the light switch. She turns the lights on. She carries a handbag

Jennifer I say, this is rather better than I expected! (*She wanders around the room and opens the french window*)

Jennifer exits to the kitchen

Brian enters L, carrying two suitcases. He sets them down, looking puzzled

(*Off*) Darling, this is heavenly . . .

Jennifer enters R

There's a terrific sunset out the back, come and see . . . what is it?
Brian Mm? Oh . . . er . . . nothing. Just that taxi driver.
Jennifer Oh him, the epitome of gloom if you ask me. I know Italian taxi drivers are supposed to talk AT you non-stop, but he's the wildest exception I've ever come across. Not a word the whole journey. Perhaps his mother just died!
Brian He didn't take the fare.
Jennifer Why not?
Brian I've no idea. He took the cases out of the back, got into the driver's seat and drove off . . . without a word.
Jennifer Maybe he was feeling generous.
Brian Mm!
Jennifer Or perhaps his mother-in-law just died!
Brian Jennifer!
Jennifer Well it's probably part of the package.

Brian What?

Jennifer Package, darling! The price ... the cost of the holiday ... all inclusive, yes?

Brian Yes, yes ... I suppose that's it.

Jennifer There you are then. Anyway we shan't need taxis any more ... when's the hire-car coming?

Brian Should be here first thing in the morning.

Jennifer Why don't you take the cases to the bedroom!

Brian Where is it?

Jennifer I should imagine it's upstairs, darling. I believe that's how houses are usually laid out ... even in Italy.

Brian Yes. ...

Brian exits L

Jennifer looks around the room at the furniture, picking up various articles and magazines. She takes a compact from her handbag and powders her nose, then lights a cigarette. Eventually she finds herself at the cocktail cabinet and examines each of the bottles there in turn

Jennifer We're in luck!

Brian returns L

Brian There's two bedrooms up there. I don't know which one you'd prefer. I put the cases in the first one.

Jennifer You mean we have a choice? I'm beginning to like this place more and more. Pour me a drink would you darling?

Jennifer exits to the hall

Brian watches her go, then looks carefully around. He switches on the table lamp and moves to the cocktail cabinet. He takes a gun from his pocket and places it carefully in the drawer. The lights flicker, dim and come up. Brian notices but does nothing. He pours a bourbon and a measure of Dubonnet

Brian exits to the kitchen for ice, taking the glasses with him

Jennifer enters from the hall

Jennifer Darling ... ! Brian?

Brian (*off*) In the kitchen!

Jennifer Darling this place is ideal. There are even two bathrooms—one each. We could have a row and sleep in separate rooms, just like home!

Brian enters R

Brian Here. ...

Jennifer Cheers! Did you notice anything about the cocktail bar.

Brian No. I mean I didn't expect any booze to be laid on but ... er ...

Jennifer But darling, I drink Dubonnet ... you drink bourbon ... they just happen to be laid on. Now isn't that nice? What did you do? Give the travel agents a rundown on our personal drinking habits?

Brian Of course not! There's other drinks besides ... (*He examines the bottles*) ... Irish whiskey, apple juice and Perrier water. Rather an odd collection, I must say. All part of the package, I suppose.

Jennifer More likely they were left by the previous occupants. Maybe they had a party; everybody drank the scotch, gin and vodka and left the rest. Must've been a wow!

Brian Why do you say that?

Jennifer Well, obviously they didn't invite any Irishmen, teetotallers ... (*she raises her glass*) bored housewives or ... (*she points to his glass*) failed TV executives.

Brian You can be very cruel sometimes.

Jennifer My darling, you've been sacked by two television companies to date, that hardly qualifies you as Businessman of the Year.

Brian As I've already told you, I'm working on a few projects; one in particular could prove highly lucrative.

Jennifer Lucrative for whom? You or the other party?

Brian May we change the subject, please?

Jennifer No. I don't think I will. I want to know more about this mysterious partner of yours. A Greek shipping tycoon, I think you said. I mean, who is he?

Brian A Greek shipping tycoon!

Jennifer Very droll, darling, very droll. But what's his name?

Brian Konakis.

Jennifer Oh yes, Konakis. But why does he want to back one of your tinpot schemes. Got money to burn, has he?

Brian It is NOT tinpot, and it is NOT one of my schemes. It was entirely his idea.

Jennifer Oh Brian! You're being taken for a ride again.

Brian Not a bit of it! It's a very sound business deal. A simple matter of importing video films. There are advantages on both sides, of course. But my end in particular will be highly profitable.

Jennifer Really! So when do we get to meet him?

Brian I told you. On Friday in Rome.

Jennifer But why do I have to go? Why can't I stay here?

Brian He particularly wants to meet you.

Jennifer Why?

Brian I don't know. He was ... very insistent. I didn't think you'd mind.

Jennifer Well I do!

Brian Now look, Jenny. We came away on this holiday to try and patch up our marriage. Or at least, find out if there's anything left to patch up. We're not doing very well so far, are we? Now let's forget about my work, or lack of it. Let's forget about our money troubles ... let's just try and ... I was going to say enjoy ourselves but perhaps that's being a bit too optimistic. (*After a pause*) How about something to eat? That airline food was appalling ... you ate even less than I did. You must be starving. The freezer's fully stocked ... I had a look ... part of the package, too, I suppose.

Jennifer Brian, are you sure we can pay for all this? This place must be costing far more than you're letting on. We're up to our eyes in debt already, you know!

Brian We can afford it.

Jennifer At the moment we can't afford anything!

Brian Look, once this deal gets off the ground, the profits will more than cover the cost of this trip in the first week.

Jennifer What profits!

Brian All right, all right! (*After a pause*) OK, you might as well know now ... you'll have to know sooner or later ... Konakis is paying for all this ... plane tickets, the villa, everything ... the taxi too, I suppose! (*He smiles*)

Jennifer turns away in disgust

It's his villa ... he owns it ... he was so pleased to finalize the deal ... it was a sort of bonus, he said.

Jennifer Oh Brian, Brian! How can you be so blind. If he's laying out all this money ... don't you see ... he must be priming you for something!

Brian Jennifer, please! Leave it to me ... trust me ... I know what I'm doing.

Jennifer Oh I don't know!

Pause

Brian How about that food, eh? What do you say?

Jennifer OK ... Brian, I'm sorry. I don't know why I laid into you like that. Force of habit, I suppose. (*She starts to go, then stops*) What a terrible thing to have to admit!

David (*off*) Someone must have left the lights on ...

Sound of a key in the front door and the door opening

Brian and Jennifer turn to the hall in surprise

David enters L, key in hand. He wears glasses

David Oh, I say ... I'm so sorry ... I must have the wrong house ... (*He looks at his key, puzzled*)

Brian Can we ... help you?

David Oh, you're English! Well, I'm sorry ... I thought this was the Villa Romana.

Jennifer This is the Villa Romana.

David Oh ... well, yes ... (*He indicates the key*) I suppose it must be, mustn't it?

Corinne enters L

Corinne Is something wrong, dear?

David Well I'm not sure ... these people seem to be ... um ...!

Brian Were you expecting to find someone else?

David No, no, not at all. Quite the opposite, really. We weren't expecting to find anybody. You see ... we've just arrived ... on holiday. We've rented this villa for two weeks ... or so we thought.

Jennifer (*to Brian*) But you said . . .

Brian I know what I said, Jenny.

David This is the Via Benario, isn't it?

Brian Yes it is the Via Benario and this is the Villa Romana. But I'm afraid you've made an unfortunate mistake. This property is privately owned and to my knowledge has never been rented out as a holiday let.

Jennifer I'm sure we can sort this out, Brian. Would either of you care for a drink?

David Thank you, no. We don't drink. Alcohol, that is.

Jennifer We have some apple juice.

Corinne Oh, that would be lovely, thank you.

Jennifer How about you Mr . . . er . . .

David Oh, I'm sorry . . . my name's Lacey . . . David Lacey . . . Corinne, my wife!

Brian Brian Stevens . . . my wife Jennifer.

Corinne Hallo!

Jennifer How do you do? (*She raises the bottle of apple juice*) . . . Er . . . Mr Lacey?

David Thank you, no. I only drink mineral water.

Jennifer Really . . .? Perrier?

David If you have some.

Jennifer Oh yes . . . (*she looks at Brian*) . . . we have some all right! (*She pours the drinks*)

David Perhaps I didn't make myself clear . . . we were lent this villa . . . by a friend of mine . . . well . . . business acquaintance . . . he owns it.

Brian Indeed? Do you mind if I ask you his name?

David Well I'd rather not if you don't mind . . . matter of professional confidentiality . . . you know how it is.

Brian No . . . I'm afraid I don't know how it is.

Corinne What my husband means Mr Stevens is that he was given the use of this villa as a bribe.

David Corinne . . . please!

Corinne Well it's the truth, isn't it?

David You must forgive my wife . . . it's not like that at all . . . it was merely a token . . . a token of thanks . . . for er . . .

Corinne For services rendered!

David Well . . . you know how it is.

Jennifer (*handing the drinks to David and Corinne*) Tell me Mr Lacey . . . this business acquaintance of yours . . . is his name by any chance . . . Konakis?

David How . . . did you know that?

Jennifer Oh . . . just a wild guess!

Brian Do you have a car outside?

Corinne No, we came by taxi. They're bringing us a hire-car sometime tomorrow.

Jennifer Brian, darling, I've suddenly acquired a ghastly headache. . . . I think I'll go and lie down for a while. It might be a good idea if you and

Mr Lacy tried to contact Mr Konakis, don't you think? Perhaps he can explain what the hell is going on!

The lights flicker, dim and come up again. They all take notice of this for a moment

Hang on in there, generator! (*She starts to leave, then turns back*) Oh by the way, do feel free to stay the night if you wish, there is a spare bedroom upstairs. I'd hate you to think that we would turn you out into the night. Will you excuse me?

Jennifer exits L

David You know Mr Konakis?

Brian I'll be back in a moment. (*He crosses to the hall and turns*) Do help yourselves to a drink, if you wish!

Brian exits L

Corinne Oh God, this is all we need.

David Did you have to blurt it out like that?

Corinne If you're ashamed, David . . .

David I am not ashamed and it is NOT a bribe . . . he was merely thankful for the . . . help and advice I was able to give him.

Corinne That still amounts to corruption, in my opinion.

David Nobody's interested in your opinion . . . in future keep it to yourself. We don't want the whole world to know.

Corinne Why not . . . if it's all so innocent?

David It can easily be misconstrued. If the Council took your view of it, it could cost me my job.

Corinne I know.

David So no more outbursts . . . please! (*After a pause*) I wonder where those two fit in.

Corinne Perhaps he's another corrupt local councillor . . .

David looks at her

Sorry!

David Maybe he's part of Konakis' organization?

Corinne What is his organization?

David I don't know for sure. He's got a lot of fingers in a lot of pies from what I can make out.

Brian enters L

Brian Sorry about that . . . so . . .! It would appear that our Mr Konakis has . . . shall we say . . . "double booked" his villa. Have you any idea where we can contact him . . . tonight, that is . . . on the telephone.

David No, I'm afraid not. I didn't think I'd have any reason to.

Brian Quite. Me neither. Not until Friday, that is. I'm meeting him in Rome.

David Oh . . . not for three days . . . how unfortunate.

Brian Yes, isn't it.

David What do you suggest we do?

Brian There's nothing we can do ... tonight. I suggest we sleep on it and in the morning I'll ring London and ... er ... see if I can find out where he is. Perhaps ... you could do the same.

David Yes, yes, of course.

Brian Good ... meanwhile if you'd care to unpack I suggest you take the room at the end of the corridor upstairs.

Corinne Thank you.

Brian One more thing. ... What's he like ...? Konakis ... as a man, I mean?

David You've ... never met him?

Brian No, not yet. We have a business deal going but so far it's all been done by correspondence. I'm meeting him for the first time on Friday.

David (*staring for a moment, then looking away*) I see.

Brian You still haven't answered my question!

Corinne My husband has never met him either. It was all done through a middleman ... an agent in England.

Brian Is that so? Oh well ... it's not important.

Sound of the front door bell

More company? Will you excuse me?

Brian exits L

David and Corinne look at each other

Franco (*off*) Scuse signor, mea automobile ...

Brian (*off*) I'm sorry, I don't speak Italian ...

Franco (*off*) Oh, you are English, yes? Scuse, signor ... my car ... she has broken down ... may I use your telephone?

Brian (*off*) Yes, I suppose so ... come in.

Franco (*off*) Grazie!

Franco enters L

Franco Oh, scuse signora ... signor ... I apologize ... my car ... she has ... how you say ... flat tyre ... two flat tyre ... glass all across road ... I have not enough tyre to replace ... so I come to use your telephone ...

Brian enters L

Brian It's in the hall there ... help yourself.

Franco Grazie, signor!

Franco exits L

There is an uncomfortable pause

Brian By the way ... there's plenty of food in the kitchen ... if you feel hungry ... please!

Corinne Thank you.

Pause

Franco returns L

Franco Scuse signor, but your telephone ... she is not working.
Brian What?
Franco There is nothing!
David Here let me try!

David exits L, *impatiently*

Franco This is most unfortunate ... there is no other ... long way to the next villa ... is possible you could drive me?
Brian We have no transport, I'm afraid. Couldn't you flag down another car?
Franco There is no traffic on this road ... road finishes at top of hill.
Brian You mean it's a dead end?
Franco Signor?
Brian Never mind.
Corinne Then what are you doing on this road? If you don't mind me asking.
Franco My business ... I sell houses ... I have appointment to meet customer at villa top of hill ... it is for sale. But he not arrive ... so I leave ... then I hit broken glass on road near here. Is good for me you are at home!
Brian Yes, wasn't it.

David enters L

David It's dead all right. The cord's been ripped out at the floor.
Brian How odd! I wonder how that could've happened. (*After a pause*) Well, it would appear you're stranded here ... at least for the moment Mr ... er ...
Franco Please ... call me Franco.
Brian Yes, well ... would you care for a drink ... my friend? I'm afraid we can't offer you very much.
Franco Thank you, no ... I have a weakness only for whiskey ... Irish whiskey ... a "hangover" from my days in England. (*He laughs*)
Brian Somehow I was afraid you were going to say that. We do have Irish whiskey Mr ... er ... may I pour you a glass?
Franco You are most kind signor, but at the moment, no thank you.
Brian As you wish. (*He pours himself another bourbon*) Tell me Mrs Lacey ... do you drink apple juice ... frequently?
Corinne Quite a lot, yes ... I happen to like it.
Brian That's what I thought.
David Why do you ask?
Brian When my wife and I arrived here this evening there were five bottles on the cocktail cabinet, only five. Bourbon, Dubonnet, apple juice, Perrier water and ... Irish whiskey. I drink bourbon ... Jennifer drinks Dubonnet ... and the others ... well ... it would appear somebody knew the five of us would be together in this house tonight ... and wanted us to feel at home!

David Coincidence!

Brian is it . . .? er . . . Franco . . . this customer of yours who failed to appear . . . did he leave a name?

Franco Si, si . . . I have it here. (*He takes a slip of paper from his pocket*) . . . er . . . Signor Konakis!

Brian Still a coincidence, Mr Lacey?

David If you'll excuse me, I'll take our cases up.

David exits L

Brian Did you speak to him personally?

Franco No, no . . . my secretary . . . she speak.

Corinne I'm beginning to feel decidedly uncomfortable.

Brian I've felt a damn sight more than that . . . since I walked into this place.

Franco There is something wrong?

Brian You could say that, my friend . . . quite what I'm not altogether sure.

Franco You . . . you know this Signor Konakis?

Brian I thought we did. Suddenly I don't think we know him at all.

David returns, holding a piece of paper and a blood-stained dagger

Corinne David?

David The . . . front door was ajar . . . there's a dead fox lying on the step outside . . . this dagger was . . .

Brian (*taking the dagger*) What's that paper?

David Oh . . . this was there, too . . . there's writing on it.

Brian (*taking the note and reading it*) "Confess your sins and you will be saved, K X."

David What does it mean?

Brian I've no idea.

Corinne Let me see! (*She examines the note*) Looks like a biblical quotation of some kind . . . "Confess your sins and you will be saved, K X" . . . Book of Kings . . . Chapter Ten . . . something like that?

Brian I don't think so . . . the X is underneath the K. (*He places the dagger on the table and examines the note further*)

David I don't wish to frighten you, but . . . the animal . . . its stomach was slit open . . . end to end!

Corinne and Franco look at him

Brian An X or "Cross" . . . when you're writing a letter . . . means a kiss, doesn't it?

Corinne So?

Brian Well . . . K . . . on . . . a kiss . . . Konakis!

David Oh now, come on!

Brian No?

David I hardly think so!

Brian Maybe not . . . and yet . . .

Pause

David I'm going upstairs. You coming, Corinne?

Corinne I'll ... be along in a minute.

David exits L

Brian places the note next to the dagger

Franco This is all most strange. I think is best ... I remove from outside ... yes?
Brian Thank you ... yes.
Franco Scuse!

Franco exits L

Corinne Do you think Konakis ...?
Brian Right now I don't think anything Mrs Lacey. (*After a pause*) If you don't mind me asking ... why did you say your husband was given the use of this villa as a ...?
Corinne As a bribe? Because that's exactly what it is. Back in England David is chairman of the planning committee on our local council. They're going to build a new civic centre ... the contract went out to tender ... Konakis put in a bid ... David has a lot of influence over the final decision ...
Brian And you don't approve?
Corinne I do not!
Brian Mm! Well ... Konakis has lent US the villa, too. But I don't think by any stretch of the imagination you could call it a bribe ... an incentive, yes! But an incentive to what ...? I'm beginning to wonder!

David comes rushing in. He is out of breath

David Mr Stevens ...! I'm sorry ... it's your wife ...
Brian Is she all right?
David I stepped into your room by mistake ... at first I thought she was asleep lying on the bed ... there was a pillow over her head ... when I lifted it off ... her eyes were open, but ...

Brian rushes past him into the hall

(*shouting*) But she's not breathing, man!
Corinne What?
David She's not breathing ... there's no pulse ... she's dead, Corinne, dead!
Corinne Are you sure?
David Of course I'm sure! Do you think I'd make a mistake about a thing like that?

Franco enters L

Franco What is happening?
David I don't know ... the lady upstairs ... I don't know ...
Corinne Shouldn't you have gone with him?
David Well ... I ...
Franco Is all right ... I go!

Franco exits L

Corinne But ... how? Why?

David How do I know!

Corinne You mean she was ... murdered?

David Look, Corinne, I don't know I tell you! There was a pillow over her head ... her eyes wide open ... a contorted expression on her face ... she must've been ... suffocated ... I don't know!

Corinne By whom ...? We must do something ... can't we call the police?

David The phone isn't working!

Corinne Well we can't just stand here ... we must go and get help!

David What do you propose? We walk ten miles down this lane to the town ...? We've no car ... it's pitch black out there.

Corinne There must be another house nearby.

David Not one building after we left the main road.

Corinne What then?

David We'll just have to wait till daylight ... there's nothing else we can do. Oh God! When the newspapers get hold of this it'll ALL come out. I'll be ruined!

Corinne Is that all you can think about?

David Right now that seems to me to be the most important consideration.

Corinne Oh really ... and what about that note from Konakis ... "confess your sins and you will be saved" ... poor Mrs Stevens wasn't saved, was she?

David What's that supposed to mean?

Corinne Maybe if she'd confessed her sins, whatever they may have been, she'd be standing here right now!

David Don't be stupid ...

Corinne So you think it's stupid, eh? What makes you think you're going to be around to be ruined, my darling? If I were you ... I'd start confessing YOUR sins ... and fast!

Franco enters L *with his arm around Brian, who is in a state of shock*

Franco Come ...!

Franco helps Brian to the sofa. Brian sits motionless with his head in his hands

Brian (*softly*) I can't believe it ... I can't believe it!

Franco The signor ... he is in a state of shock. Perhaps ... some strong drink?

David Of course! (*He crosses to the cocktail cabinet and, without thinking, pours a glass of Irish whiskey*)

Franco The lady ... has been ... how you say ...

Corinne Yes ... we know ...

Franco Ah ... si ...

David gives the glass to Franco, who offers it to Brian

Signor!

Brian takes it and drinks

It would appear we can do nothing tonight. We must wait till morning. I suggest ... signora ... signor ... you go to your room and ... try to get some rest. I will stay here with your friend.

Corinne You think we can sleep after what's happened?

Franco Please signora ... I think it best your friend is left alone ... what he needs is peace and quiet ... I will stay ... only to keep an eye on him ... please!

David and Corinne, suspicious of Franco, glance at each other

David Yes, yes ... of course ... perhaps that would be for the best ... Corinne?

David exits

Corinne Thank you for ... er ... well, thank you!

Franco smiles

Corinne exits L

Franco (*standing by Brian*) Drink, signor ... it is good for you.

Brian Yes ... yes ... (*He drains the glass*)

Franco Good! (*He takes the glass, crosses to the cocktail cabinet and pours a large measure of Irish whiskey. He returns to Brian*) Come signor! You will feel much better.

Brian takes the glass and drinks

Good! That is ... ve-ery good! (*He picks up the note from the table and studies it. Then he picks up the dagger*) It deadens the pain ... does it not?

Black-out

CURTAIN

SCENE 2

The same. Later that evening

As the CURTAIN *rises Brian is lying stretched out on the sofa, facing upstage and covered by a rug. His jacket lies draped over the back of the sofa. Franco is sitting in the chair apparently asleep. The french window curtains are now closed and the stage is in darkness apart from a spill of light from the hall*

After a moment David appears in the archway. He is wearing a dressing-gown over his shirt and trousers. He surveys the room, then crosses quietly to the kitchen and turns on the kitchen light

Franco Signor ...

David Oh ... I'm sorry ... I thought you were asleep.

Franco No, signor ... sleep comes very difficult.

David I know what you mean ... we've been awake, too. How is Mr Stevens?

Franco (*switching on the lamp beside the chair*) He was restless for some time

... but now he sleep like a baby ... how you say ... dead to the world.

David Just as well, I suppose. Look ... er ... my wife and I have been talking this over ... I mean ... it's pretty obvious that Konakis intended for all five of us to end up here tonight. The question is ... why?

Franco I agree with you, signor. It no accident that I am here ... I am sure of that.

David The point is ... if that note did come from Konakis ... and I must admit, it is a possibility ... and if he did kill Mrs Stevens ... then maybe ... I know it sounds incredible ... but maybe ... he intends to kill us all!

Franco (*picking up the note and looking at it*) That thought has occurred to me, signor.

David Then you must see! "Confess your sins and you will be saved" ... he's obviously trying to tell us something, to warn us in advance ... if we confess our sins ... then he won't kill us.

Franco I am ahead of you, Signor. But sins against whom ...? Against HIM ...? I do not know him.

David That's just it ... nor do we ... none of us do! None of us have ever met him! But what if he's an impostor ... what if Konakis is not his real name ... what if he's not even a Greek? But somebody entirely different using the name Konakis as a cover ... somebody we DO all know!

Franco But you people are from England ... I have not met any of you before. I live here, in Italy.

David Yes, but didn't you say something about "your time in England".

Franco Is true ... I spend two years in London as a student, many years ago.

David Well don't you see ...? He could be someone we all know back in the UK ... someone from our past ... that we sinned against, double-crossed in some way ... and now he's seeking revenge.

Franco Is possible ...

David Oh it's more than that ... I'm sure of it ... and we have one way out ... if we admit ... openly ... how we wronged him ... then he'll spare us. "Confess your sins and you will be saved!"

Franco How can we do that? We don't know who he is ... or what we did!

David We must think ... fast ... all of us ... everybody we've harmed ... however remotely! Come on, let's wake him up!

Franco But he needs to rest.

David Unless we come up with Konakis' true identity, one of us will be taking a longer rest than he bargained for!

Franco Yes, you are right!

David (*shaking Brian*) Mr Stevens ... Brian. ... (*He places his hand on Brian's cheek*) Mr Stevens ...! (*He removes his hand quickly*) My God ...! He's as cold as ice!

Franco pushes David aside, feels Brian's cheek, lifts his eyelids, feels his pulse

Franco (*softly*) Mama mia! (*He bends closer to Brian's face and sniffs*) ... mandorla!

David What?

Franco Almonds ... the smell of almonds ... cyanide!

David (*softly*) Oh, no!

They look at each other, then to the hallway, then back at each other. There is an uncomfortable pause

I thought I heard . . . my wife coming downstairs, excuse me!

He exits awkwardly through the hallway. He returns shortly after, shrugs his shoulders and shakes his head

Pause

Franco/Frank Oh, hell . . .! Corinne!

He exits L

(*Off*) Angela . . .! Angela!

Frank returns. There is a pause while he decides what to do. He looks at his watch

OK Pamela . . . we'll call a halt there. Angela is OFF! Do you hear me, Pam?

Pamela (*off*) Coming!

Frank Just relax, Derek. We'll start the scene again from the top . . . WHEN she appears.

Pamela enters. She is a prim lady with her hair tied back. She wears glasses

Pamela Yes Frank? (*She is holding a script of the play with a newspaper on top. She is concentrating on the crossword*)

Frank See if you can find Angela, will you? She's missed her entrance AGAIN! And leave the crossword for the moment, will you?

Pamela Sorry!

She places the script, newspaper and pen on the table behind the sofa and exits to the kitchen

Frank (*removing sheaves of paper from his pocket*) Might as well give a few notes as we've ground to a halt . . . (*He shouts*) And Pam! Bang the lights up for a moment, will you love!

Pamela (*off*) OK!

Frank Now let me see . . . er . . . where are we . . .? Scene one . . . (*He thumbs through his notes*)

Brian/Martin raises himself very slowly to a sitting position. His face is pale with make-up. Once upright, he speaks

Brian/Martin Mind if I get up?

Frank No, feel free. At the moment the play is deader than you are.

Pause. The remainder of the stage lights come up

David/Derek (*sitting in the chair and removing his glasses*) Did you have to employ that woman?

Frank Derek, I know how you feel and I'm sorry; but we're stuck with her. She's a good actress when she tries.

Derek WHEN she tries!

Frank Now ... where was I ...? er ... first of all ... you're all rushing it ... just a little. Enjoy it ... give the audience time ... there's a lot happens in that first scene ... we don't want them to miss any of the important points ... let the plot unfold naturally. ...

Derek What plot?

Frank Pass that on to the girls, will you ...? Er. ... Yes. ... Martin ...! (*He searches for words*) ... you're making Brian too sinister ... we don't need it ... relax a bit ... he's coming across guilty as hell at the moment ... you'll have the audience thinking you're Konakis or something. ...

Martin That's what I want them to think!

Frank No, no ... too much, too much ... tone it down a bit ... er ... (*He crosses out a few lines*) ... Oh, these lights ... honestly!

Martin The flickering gremlins!

Frank We've got to do something about that. Now where's that damn lighting board?

Frank exits L

Pause

Derek I don't know why I took this job. I could be sitting snugly at home ... watching TV ... drawing the dole ... not a care in the world.

Martin Why is it that actors are so utterly depressed when they're out of work, yet are the first to complain when they get a job?

Derek Nature of the breed, dear boy.

Martin Well I don't mind admitting, I'm grateful for any work these days.

Derek Not exactly the big time, though, is it? Ten days rehearsal and only one performance. Do we know who's going to be out there, yet? (*He indicates the auditorium*)

Martin Haven't a clue! Just the author and a few of his friends, according to Frank.

Derek (*enthusiastically*) I wonder if he's invited any West End managements!

Martin You never know your luck. Mind you, I shouldn't think any of them would touch it, it's not that good a play, you know!

Derek Too right!

Martin Well I'm not complaining. As long as we get paid.

Derek He must be worth a bob or two ... a country house like this with its own private little theatre.

Martin Doesn't seem to use it much ... the place is deserted. Maybe he comes for weekends.

Derek (*sarcastically*) A weekend cottage in the country. How naice!

Martin Spot of fishing ... a stroll round the estate.

Derek Ride with the local hunt. ...

Martin Debutantes for tea. ...

Derek (*correcting him*) Crumpet for tea!

Martin Same thing!

They laugh

You know ... he could have his own little fringe theatre here.
Derek Fringe theatre?
Martin Why not?
Derek This place is so far out on the "fringe" ... you'd fall off the edge!

*The french window curtains open suddenly. Jennifer/Kate is standing there.
She is wearing a dressing-gown*

Jennifer/Kate Is this a private party or can anyone join?
Derek Angela's done her disappearing act again.
Kate Oh terrific!
Derek At this rate we'll still be doing this turgid dress rehearsal when old
Leadwood takes his seat in the Royal Box. (*He indicates the auditorium*)
Kate Perhaps he's already out there! (*She walks quickly downstage and
speaks out front*) Coo-ee ... Mr Leadwood ... are you there?

Frank enters L*; he is apparently looking for Pamela*

It's Kate Brotherston ... "Star of the Show" ... I can do a quick cancan
while we're waiting, if you like? (*She hitches up her dressing-gown*)
Frank Kate ... please ... would you mind!
Kate Yes sir ... sorry Mr Director, sir!
Derek (*teasing her*) Careful, Kate ... he might be listening.
Kate I don't care! And I'm sure our nice Mr Leadwood doesn't mind ...
after all, he is paying us to entertain him for the evening.
Derek Kate, really ... sometimes you can be so. ...
Kate Embarrassing? Yes, I know ... isn't it fun? (*She notices Martin for the
first time*) Martin ...! What on earth have you done to yourself?
Martin Mm? Oh this. (*He touches his face*) It's make-up. I thought I ought
to look like a corpse.
Kate You look positively decomposed!

Pamela enters R

Pamela (*in a bored tone*) She isn't in her dressing-room or the men's
dressing-room.
Derek You mean you've been all this time doing that?
Pamela I went to the loo!
Kate First night nerves, is it dear?
Derek I should look further afield if I were you. She's probably wandered
off into the house somewhere.
Kate On the look-out for antiques, no doubt. You know what she's like!

Pamela looks at Frank, who nods for her to go

Pamela (*reluctantly*) OK.

Pamela exits L

Martin May I make a suggestion?
Kate Martin ...! Darling ...! I thought you were dead! Oh no, that's in the
play isn't it? So sorry. Do go on.

Derek You're dead, too, remember. Unfortunately that's only in the play as well.

Frank Whatever it is you want to say, Martin, do say it now and stop these two from talking, for Pete's sake!

Martin Well it seems to me ... we're wasting valuable time. Couldn't we cut Angela's scene for the moment, and carry on with the next one. Otherwise we'll never get through the dress rehearsal.

Kate Mm! Who's the conscientious one, then?

Frank Look we'll give Angela another couple of minutes. If she turns up, give me a shout, will you? I'm going to take another look at that lighting board ... must be a loose connection somewhere! Derek ... would you mind giving me a hand? You know a thing or two about electrics. ...

Derek Sure ... cost you double time, though!

Frank exits L

Oh ... by the way, Frank ...

Derek exits L

Pause

Kate (*restlessly picking up Pamela's newspaper*) Come along, Martin ...! Let's improve our minds! (*She refers to the crossword*) "One prune extremely wrinkled wasn't ready for picking" ... six letters. "One prune ... extremely wrinkled" ... sounds like Pamela!

Martin Unripe.

Kate Come again.

Martin Unripe. It's an anagram of the figure one and prune.

Kate Mm! (*She tosses down the newspaper*) Unripe, eh? Sounds like me. (*She picks up Pamela's script*)

Martin More like overripe!

Kate Now, now! I think I'm very well preserved. Good, clean living ... that's what does it. My mother always used to say to me; "Now remember, Katy, if you're not in bed by eleven ... come home!" (*She laughs, then after a pause, reads aloud the title page*) The Domino Man by Arthur Leadwood! Yuk! What does it mean?

Martin What does that mean?

Kate (*turning up her nose*) The Domino Man.

Martin You mean you've been rehearsing this play for ten days and you don't know what the title means.

Kate Darling! More often than not I speak LINES and I don't know what they mean!

Martin (*laughing*) The domino is the long cloak with the hood, ... that people ...

Kate Oh, that thing Derek wears at the end of the play. ...

Martin That's right! People used to wear them to masked balls to conceal their identity. *The Domino Man* simply means a man in disguise.

Kate Which is David Lacey, right?

Martin Well, sort of! The real Domino Man is Konakis.

Kate (*not understanding*) Why?

Martin (*as if explaining to a child*) Because Konakis is not his real name . . . and he's not a Greek . . . he's someone completely different . . . a man in disguise!

Kate Oh yes . . . (*She is unimpressed*) Clever! (*After a pause*) What do you think of it . . . as a play?

Martin Well I've seen better . . . I suppose it's not a bad little thriller. What about you?

Kate I think it's crummy!

Martin Why?

Kate Well, I mean . . . really! Five people are lured to a remote Italian villa where they're all done in one by one . . . until at the end one of them is apparently resurrected and turns out to be the murderer. It's not exactly original . . . it's straight out of Agatha Christie!

Martin Mm! It's a crib, yes . . . but not a straight crib. I mean . . . Lacey is working for Konakis, who is not . . .

Kate Who is not Konakis at all! My! But how ingenious! It'll run longer than *The Mousetrap*.

Martin So why did you take the job?

Kate (*shrugging*) I've been out of work six months . . . I've been waitressing in Covent Garden since March . . . anything . . . ANYTHING to get away from having my bottom pinched twenty times a day.

Martin I'd have thought you would've enjoyed that.

Kate (*genuinely hurt*) Oh Martin . . .! If only you knew. Well . . . that's the image I present I suppose, isn't it? My own fault really. If the truth were known, I'm not like that at all . . . basically, I'm a nice person.

Martin I believe you.

Kate That's another thing about this play. They're all such AWFUL people . . . they deserve to get bumped off. Why don't they write plays about NICE people any more? I think plays should be romantic . . . two people meet and fall in love . . . they get married and have lots of kids. Now don't laugh! I like that sort of thing, that's why I like old movies, I suppose. I just love sitting curled up on the sofa watching Doris Day on a Saturday afternoon. You know . . . when I was a kid . . . I wanted so much to live in that world . . . the white, weather boarded house . . . with the white picket fence running round the edge of the garden . . . roses growing up the balcony . . . and the sky permanently blue!

Martin smiles

Oh, I knew it wasn't real. I knew it was all built of plywood, or what have you . . . I knew the roses were plastic and the sky was a painted backcloth . . . I KNEW it was all inside a film studio! But I still wanted to live there. Do you think that's silly?

Martin No.

Kate So I became an actress. I wanted to be the next Doris Day . . .! Some actress . . .! It took me ten years to get into the West End. It was a good play, too . . . but do you know how long it ran? Three weeks! The reviews were terrific, business was booming, but the management took it off after three weeks. You know why? They were using it as a tax loss ... that's my luck!

Martin That's really tough. Who was the management?

Kate Howard de la Tour ... who else! The biggest crook in the business. "Howard de la Whore" we used to call him ... he'd sell anything for money! Have you ever worked for him?

Martin No.

Kate Well don't bother ... it's slave labour.

Martin I thought he'd gone out of busines, anyway ... fled the country, or something.

Kate He'll turn up somewhere. Knowing Howard he's probably touring Argentina with a production of *Anyone for Denis?*

They laugh

Pause

Well ... needless to say ... I didn't get the picket fence. Instead ... I got a bedsitter in Notting Hill ... down to earth with a bump. (*She picks up the script*) And I still say this is a crummy play! Whoever heard of an Italian who drinks Irish whiskey?

Martin You have a point there.

Kate And what about that note from Konakis? K X ... K ... on ... a kiss! I mean, really ... I've seen better riddles on a lavatory wall!

They smile

Pause

Martin Shouldn't you be helping to look for Angela?

Kate Me? Why?

Martin We want to get through the dress rehearsal, don't we?

Kate We've got hours before curtain up. Plenty of time!

Martin Even so ...

Kate Why should I go, anyway? Why not you?

Martin You are supposed to be on stage-management as well, you know.

Kate Ssh! Keep your voice down ... I'm hoping Frank's forgotten about that. You remind him ... and he'll have me making tea all night.

Martin Still ...

Kate Still, nothing! I do my bit ... I work the sound-tape ... the music cues, the whole of the storm sequence AND Konakis' voice at the end.

Martin (*melodramatically mimicking the sound-tape*) "Confess your sins and you will be saved!"

Kate (*smiling*) I'll have you know I'm highly efficient at it.

Martin I'm sure you are.

Kate I still don't see why Pamela couldn't have done it.

Martin She's doing the lighting changes.

Kate She could do both, she's capable.

Pause

Martin Did you ... mind?

Kate What?

Martin Did you mind when Frank asked you to stage-manage . . . as well as play Jennifer?

Kate It hurt to the quick, I can tell you! Still . . . beggars can't be choosers . . . Jennifer is only a bit part . . . I had to justify my fee in some way, I suppose.

Martin I hope you don't feel . . . well . . . bitter.

Kate Oh don't get me wrong . . . I'm grateful . . . I need the work . . . truly!

Martin Yes. . . . (*After a pause*) Tell me, Kate . . . why do you dislike Derek so much?

Kate Dislike Derek! Me? Don't be silly!

Martin But you're always bitching at each other.

Kate Oh that! That's just the way we communicate. We score points off each other. We're two of a kind . . . I'm quite fond of him, really.

Martin Did you know him before . . .? Before this job, I mean.

Kate No. I knew his wife, though. We worked together at Salisbury rep earlier this year . . . Rebecca . . .! Extremely pretty girl . . . damn her eyes! (*Quietly*) I hear tell she left him recently. I know for a fact she was having an affair down at Salisbury. Nobody in the company, mind . . . but she was always sneaking off somewhere or other to meet this . . . er . . . secret beau of hers. She must've been out of her mind.

Martin Why?

Kate Well . . . I mean . . . Derek's quite good-looking in a way, don't you think?

Martin I wouldn't know.

Kate I think Pamela's got her eye on him.

Martin What . . . Derek?

Kate Ah-ha!

Martin I hardly think so.

Kate Oh yes, there's more to Miss Pamela Fox than meets the eye.

Martin She spends all her time avoiding him, from what I can see.

Kate Exactly! She's playing hard to get.

Martin laughs

No, it's true. You may scoff! Didn't you notice on the way down in the minibus . . . she insisted on sitting in the front seat? Why? Because Derek was sitting there.

Martin She sat in the front because she gets car sick.

Kate Rubbish! She's making a play for him. I should know, I've done it often enough.

Martin Ah, now we get down to the nitty-gritty . . .

Kate Oh Martin, do wipe that make-up off your face . . . (*She gives him a handful of tissues from her dressing-gown pocket*) It gives me the willies every time I look at you!

Martin does so

Derek and Frank enter L

Derek ... but if I say the line as it's written, the audience will know at once that it's ME who's been knocking everybody off.

Frank Derek, we can't change any lines now ... he'll be in the audience ... he'll know we've changed it!

Derek (*backing down*) It'll give the game away ...

Frank Angela turned up yet?

Martin No, 'fraid not. Any sign of old Leadwood?

Kate We don't know that he's old. I'll bet he's frightfully attractive.

Derek To you ... all rich men are attractive.

Kate What about it, Frank? Is he dishy?

Frank You can decide for yourself tonight, can't you?

Derek He'll probably creep into the back row in the dark and creep out again as soon as the show's over. We might not even know he's been there.

Frank He's paying for the privilege.

Derek How do we know he's going to turn up? How do we know we're going to get paid?

Frank He paid me everything in advance. As soon as the curtain comes down, you'll get your money; I shall give it to you!

Derek The sooner the better, if you ask me.

Kate I don't know. I think it's all rather fun.

Derek Fun? I've had more fun at a funeral!

Kate So why did you take the job?

Derek shrugs

You needed the work as badly as the rest of us, admit it!

Derek·OK. I admit it. But I don't think he's paying us enough. We should've stuck out for more.

Martin I'm satisfied.

Derek Yes, well I'm not. He should be paying us danger money ... (*he smiles*) it's a danger to our artistic integrity to be doing such third-rate rubbish. If he can afford to waste money building a set for one night, then he can pay us a fair whack ... (*he looks around*) It's pathetic, yes, but it's a set. ... (*He chuckles*) Well it's an Italian villa ... at a pinch!

Frank Pathetic or not ... Pamela and I did the set last weekend.

Kate What, all of it?

Frank No, no ... the set itself was already here ... been here for months by the look of it ... left over from some other play ... but it served our purpose. We had to adapt it a little ... we took out a door from over there ... (*He indicates the hallway*) And gave it a coat of paint. We borrowed the furniture from the house.

Kate Ooooh ...! I hope you asked permission!

Frank I was given a free hand.

Derek (*half-heartedly*) Well I still say "there's something rotten in the State of Denmark".

Kate (*sarcastically*) Careful, darling ... he might be listening!

Derek He's probably ninety-three years old and ... (*He shouts out front*) STONE DEAF!

Kate Now we don't want to offend him, Derek dear. He might not employ us again. Be nice to our Mr Leadwood . . .! He might ask you back to play Dame in his pantomime!

Derek (*smiling*) I can see why Frank cast you in this part, Kate. Typecasting to a "T".

Kate Now don't get bitchy, darling!

Derek ME bitchy? Huh!

Kate (*flirting with Frank*) You didn't typecast me at all, now did you Frank? Strictly a character performance, isn't that so, Frank?

Frank (*studying his notes*) I didn't cast you.

Kate You didn't cast me! Then who did?

Frank Arthur Leadwood.

Kate (*flattered*) Really . . .?ˑWell now . . .! I wonder how he knows little old me.

Frank He picked all of you. Pamela as well.

Kate is deflated

Derek All of us?

Frank Yes.

Derek But you said you'd seen me on TV and that's why you wanted me for this part.

Frank Yes, I know . . . well . . . I thought it might persuade you to take the job . . . you weren't all that keen as I remember.

Derek Too right I wasn't!

Kate Frank Robinson . . .! You told a fib!

Frank Look, if I've offended you, I'm sorry. I didn't want anyone else dropping out, that's all. Simon Shaw had already withdrawn at the last minute, as you know. Otherwise I wouldn't be lumbered with playing Franco.

Kate Franco Robinsoni!

Frank gives her a withering look

Well I think your accent is terrific!

Frank Thank you.

Kate Come on, now, Derek, you should be flattered. You've got a fan club at last. Albeit with only one member.

Derek Well at least he has good taste in actors. I'm not so sure the same can be said for actresses!

Martin I wonder where Leadwood knows me from. Must've seen my baked beans commercial.

Derek He's certainly living up to his name, I know that . . . LEADen plot and WOODen dialogue!

Frank Now come along, please. You're all behaving like children. Let's just concentrate on doing the performance this evening . . . then we can all go home. It is only one performance after all.

Kate What do you think of it, Frank . . .? As a play, I mean. Come on now . . . honest opinion!

Frank (*hesitantly*) Well . . . it's not bad . . . pretty good for a first effort . . . it deserves a showing.

Derek "corpses"

Kate giggles

Frank wanders in disgust to the french windows and looks out, waiting for Angela and Pamela

Kate Do you think if I wrote him a letter saying how absolutely terrific his play is, he'd ask me to be in his next one?

Martin I doubt it.

Kate I did that once. I'd just played the girl in *What the Butler Saw* at Harrogate. So I wrote this really rambling "treacley" letter to Joe Orton saying how brilliant and fantastic his play was. Then I asked my agent if he could find out where Joe Orton lived, so I could send it to him, you see. You know what he said? "Joe Orton died ten years ago!"

Martin and Derek laugh

I was terrific in that part, too. I got a fan letter . . . a real fan letter . . . the only one I've ever had. It was from two sisters . . . there was pages and pages of it . . . with little drawings of scenes from the play . . . and flowers painted all the way up the margin. (*She giggles*) You know what their names were . . .? Lettice and Ismay Langworthby!

Martin Oh come off it, Kate!

Kate No, it's true . . . I swear it . . . absolutely true!

Derek It's a forgery, darling . . . nobody has names like that . . . it was probably written by one of the other actors in the company.

Kate (*deflated*) That's what everybody else said at the time!

Derek shakes his head in disbelief

Kate looks depressed

Martin looks in sympathy towards her

Pause

Frank (*joining them downstage*) Oh well . . . I've er . . . I've got a few more notes. By the way, Kate! I've already told the boys . . . that first scene . . . you're rushing it, just a bit. Give Brian more time in the kitchen. He's in and out like a yo-yo at the moment. He has to look in the freezer and all that business. Give the plot points a little more air . . . more space . . . play with it . . . it's all you've got so you might as well make the most of it.

Kate Now that's an offer I can't refuse.

Frank (*consulting his notes*) Derek . . . that scene with me . . . Brian on the sofa . . . just about where we stopped . . . you're hamming it a bit, old man!

Derek looks appalled

Yes . . . Kate! Now I know the facilities here are a bit primitive . . . but if the lights flicker again . . . don't say "hang on in there generator"! Please!

Kate Didn't you like it? It's a line from *Deathtrap*. I did it last year at York.
I thought it was appropriate.

Frank Yes ... well that's as maybe ... but I'd rather you didn't ad lib at all
if you don't mind. Somehow I don't think Mr Leadwood would appreciate your tampering with his lines. Anyway, we've checked the lighting
board; with any luck they won't flicker again.

Sound of a door closing

Angela?

Pamela enters thrugh the french windows

Pamela No, it's me.

Frank Well?

Pamela This place is incredible. There are endless corridors and they're all
full of paintings; there are suits of armour, swords, antique pistols ...
there's even a Persian tapestry!

Kate So it's a Sotheby's depository, dear. What about Angela?

Pamela Not a sign, she's vanished.

Frank Oh hell ...! well, er ... (*he looks at his watch*) ... er ... put the kettle
on will you love?

Pamela exits

Frank wanders disconsolately

Pause

Kate Have you noticed that whenever directors can't think of a positive
instruction to give their stage-manager ... they always send them to make
TEA?

Martin (*wandering to the archway*) I could do with something stronger.

Frank Right ...! Now, er ... we're coming up to the storm sequence in this
next scene. Now Derek, remember ... don't panic too soon ... in
yesterday's run through you anticipated you were about to be shot ...
don't! Let it come as a surprise to the audience.

Pamela screams off-stage

They all react

Martin It's OK. I'll go!

He exits L

Derek I do wish women wouldn't do that!

Kate It's all right ... Pam probably looked in a mirror by mistake.

Frank A fat lot you care. She could be hurt for all you know. (*He starts to
follow Martin*)

Derek I wouldn't be surprised if this place was haunted.

Frank confronts Martin and Pamela in the archway. Pamela is sobbing

Frank What is it?

Martin Sit her down, Frank, quick!

Martin exits L

Frank (*putting his arm around Pamela*) Pam? What's the matter, love? What is it?

She is unable to answer

(*Looking around*) Well don't just stand there, Derek!

They help Pamela to the sofa. Frank sits beside her

Don't worry, my darling, it's all over now. . . . Have either of you got any brandy, scotch . . . anything like that?

Derek (*indicating the cocktail cabinet*) Irish Whiskey?

Frank That's not funny, Derek.

Kate Don't go away!

Kate exits R

Derek Well, what happened?

Frank How do I know . . .? It's all right, Pam . . . you're OK now.

Derek Where's Martin?

Frank I don't know, he disappeared round the back again.

Kate enters R *holding a thermos flask. She pours something into the cup*

Frank What's that?

Kate Pamela's coffee . . . or so she would have us believe. Smells more like Courvoisier four-star, to me.

Kate hands the cup to Frank, who gives it to Pamela. She gulps it down quickly

Martin enters L. *He is very shaken*

Derek You look as if you've seen a ghost.

Martin It's Angela . . . she's lying stretched out on the floor of the stage-management room. (*His hand wanders involuntarily towards his neck*)

Pamela She's . . . she's dead. . . .

Pause

Kate } (*together*) { Good God!
Derek }   { What?

Pamela She's been . . . she's been strangled . . .! (*She bursts into loud sobbing*)

Black-out

CURTAIN

ACT II

Scene 1

The same. A moment later

Derek Strangled?
Frank Now come on. . . . There must be some mistake! Who on earth . . .?
Martin There's no mistake. I felt her pulse. She's dead all right.
Kate I can't believe it . . .! Angela?

Derek moves upstage

Martin I wouldn't go in there, if I were you.
Derek Don't worry, I'm not going to.
Pamela There are deep red marks on her neck . . . and . . . her eyes . . .! Oh
  my God, her eyes!
Martin I don't think any of us should go in there until the police arrive.
Derek The police?
Martin Yes.
Derek Do we have to . . .?
Kate Oh come on, Derek. We can't just ignore it, it's not going to go away!
Derek Yes, yes . . . of course . . . sorry! I wasn't thinking.
Frank Has anybody called them?
Martin (*distractedly*) No, no . . . I don't even know where the phone is . . . if
  there is one.

Pause

Kate (*to Derek*) Don't you think one of you should go and phone?
Derek Well don't look at me!
Kate Martin obviously isn't up to it!
Frank It's all right. . . . I'll go. . . . Kate! (*He indicates for her to comfort
  Pamela*) It's probably downstairs in the hallway where we came in.
Kate (*moving to Pamela*) Derek, you go with him!
Derek No thanks.
Frank It's all right, I can take care of myself.

  Frank exits R

Pause

Derek I can't believe this is happening, I mean . . .

Pause

Kate Derek! (*She indicates for him to offer the brandy flask to Martin*)

Derek (*offering the flask*) Martin, here . . .! It's brandy.
Martin Thanks. (*He takes the flask and drinks*)

Pause

Who would want to do such a thing? She was such a harmless girl.

Pause

Kate Whoever did it . . . might still be here.
Derek Exactly.
Kate Then why did you let Frank go alone?
Derek If you think I'm going to stroll about this house with a murderer on the loose, you can go whistle!

Pause

Kate You . . . knew her before, didn't you Martin?
Martin (*hesitantly*) Er . . . a little.
Kate Did she . . . have any enemies?
Martin No, no, no . . . not at all. Everybody loved her.
Pamela (*now recovered*) What makes you think he's loose in the house? It could be one of you!

The others are shocked. There is a long pause

Derek (*quietly dismissive*) That's ridiculous.
Pamela Is it so ridiculous? There's nobody else here is there . . . in the theatre, in the house?
Kate Pam . . .! Have some more brandy.
Pamela Don't patronize me, Kate!
Kate I'm not patronizing you . . .
Pamela Then don't try and change the subject. None of you liked her! All right, she was forgetful at times, so you all made fun of her behind her back. None of YOU loved her!
Kate That's just not true!
Martin Pamela . . . we've all had a terrible shock, you in particular, we know that. But let's not make wild accusations, it won't do any good.
Pamela Well I don't think it's so wild. Can any of you prove you didn't do it?
Martin Frank, Derek and I were on-stage when Angela disappeared, so it must have been you or Kate, is that what you're saying?
Derek That's true!
Kate But it's not true, not exactly. You three were on-stage when Angela "failed to appear", that's not quite the same thing. She could have been . . . well . . . it could have happened earlier.
Pamela That's right!
Martin Why would any of us want to kill Angela?
Kate Ten days ago none of us knew her. Or each other, come to that.
Pamela Martin knew her . . . he said so.
Martin But I liked her!

Derek Look, let's just cool it, shall we? Let's just wait for the police to arrive.

Pamela Oh you'd like that, wouldn't you? Give you time to invent an alibi!

Derek I don't need to invent an alibi!

Pamela Well one of you does!

Derek You exclude yourself from this little scenario, do you Pamela?

Pamela I know I didn't do it.

Derek Ha!

Kate (*quietly*) Derek!

Derek You've such an analytical mind, Pam. Too many Times crosswords. It'll be your downfall one of these days.

Kate Leave the poor girl alone! Let her have her say, if she wants to.

Pause

Martin All right, Pam ... just what is it you're trying to say?

Pause

Pamela (*more calmly*) The last time I saw Angela ... was the end of the first scene ... her exit with Derek. That's about ten minutes before her next entrance ... which is where we stopped. Any one of you might have killed her in that time.

Derek Rubbish!

Martin No, no Derek ... hold on! In theory ... Pamela is right.

Derek Now listen ...!

Martin IN THEORY ...! Now, Pam ... if we eliminate each of us ... one by one ... will that make you feel any better?

Pamela nods

OK ... Derek?

Derek What?

Martin You and Angela left the stage together ... it would appear you had the first opportunity.

Derek Thank you so much, Martin, for that kind thought!

Kate Well what did you do ... the two of you ... after you got off-stage?

Derek I don't have to answer that question!

Martin (*rising and moving to Derek*) Derek, no one's accusing you of anything! We just want to put Pamela's mind at rest. (*In a quiet voice*) Go on! (*He nods towards Pamela as if to say "for Pete's sake, humour her!"*)

Derek OK, OK ... if you want to play games. I left the stage and went straight to the dressing-room ... I have a change of costume, remember? (*He indicates his dressing-gown*) Angela was behind me ... I don't know where she went!

Martin And then?

Derek Look ... I took off my jacket and tie and put on my dressing-gown, OK? Then I sat down and ... looked at the script, I think ... yes, I ... I went over my lines for the next scene. When I heard the scene-drop music fade out, I came back to the wings and straight on-stage. And before you ask the next question ... yes, I was alone the whole time ... I saw nobody and nobody saw me, all right? So I had a solid three minutes, or whatever it was, in which to kill Angela ... is that what you wanted to hear, Pamela? Does that put your mind at rest?

Kate Derek, please ...!

Derek Three minutes, uh? Hardly enough time to kill a cat!

Pause

Martin Not necessarily! Not if you know the right pressure points on the neck ... it's all over in a matter of seconds ... even a woman could do it. She wouldn't even have screamed.

They all look at Martin suspiciously

Well don't look at me like that! It's just something I picked up ... I'm not saying I'd ever put it into practice!

Pause

Derek And what about you, Martin? Where were you?

Martin Well, I'm sorry to disappoint you ...

Derek We're all ears, dear boy!

Martin I was on-stage the whole time. I'm on at the end of scene one ... and I'm on at the beginning of scene two. During the scene change I stayed put! I simply took off my jacket, loosened my tie and lay down on the sofa. Oh, I ... I put the make-up on my face first ... I keep it in my jacket pocket ... you can check if you like! (*He indicates his jacket which is lying on the back of the sofa*) Then Pam covered me with the rug. That's how I'm discovered on curtain-up.

Derek Pam?

Pamela Yes ... yes, that's right!

Derek OK, that lets Martin off the hook. (*To Pamela*) What about yourself? "Even a woman could do it."

Pamela I was in the corner all the time.

Derek Oh, really?

Kate Oh come on, Derek, of course she was! Do you think the tabs opened and closed themselves?

Pamela Except during the scene change, of course. I was on-stage changing the props ... just a few glasses. I ... closed the curtains at the french windows and ... put the rug over Martin. Then I went back to the corner, set up the next lighting cue and stood by to open the tabs. Martin ... was here the whole time.

Derek Oh great! You're making me feel really good, you know that? And what about you Kate? Come on ... surprise me!

Kate I was in the corner, too, operating the sound tape. Pam will vouch for that.

Derek Wonderful. You've all got alibis for each other ... all except "muggins" here!

Kate That's not strictly true, Derek. If it will make you feel any easier ... as soon as scene two had begun ... I went back to my dressing room ... I was alone ... nobody saw me ... I was there ... what ...? I don't know

... five minutes? ... before you and Frank found yourselves "treading treacle"!

Derek Kate! How chivalrous of you! You've come to my rescue. What did you do ... in your dressing-room?

Kate I read my book ... but, of course, I can't prove that. That is until I heard Frank's voice shouting for Angela. Now it occurred to my tiny little mind that either Frank had written in a new scene or the dress rehearsal had come to a standstill! So I came to investigate.

Derek Thank you Kate. Now ... what book were you reading?

Kate Oh, Derek ... really!!

Derek No, come on ... try me!

Kate Forget it!

Derek Can't you remember?

Kate It's called *Beyond Belief*!

Derek (*laughing*) Oh boy ...! That just about sums up this whole situation!

Pamela How can you make fun at a time like this?

Derek We have to get through the rest of today somehow!

Pause

Kate What about Frank? What were his movements?

Pause

Derek Does anybody know?

Martin Well ... now you mention it ... it was rather odd.

Derek What was?

Martin Well ... Frank is on-stage the same as me ... end of scene one ... beginning of scene two ... but during the scene change ... well, as soon as the tabs closed ... he disappeared off-stage rather sharpish.

Pamela Yes, that's right ... he brushed past me as I came on with the rug.

Martin I remember he didn't appear again until the very last second. I thought HE was going to be off. Eventually he ran on ... loosened his tie, tousled his hair, and flopped down in the chair ... you know, as if Franco had been asleep. He was definitely out of breath. I remember because ... I thought at the time ... the audience would hardly believe he'd been sleeping ... if he was ... out of breath!

Derek So! That would have given him, what ...? A minute ...? Minute and a half?

Pamela The scene change was two minutes ... I timed it.

Derek The "two-minute murderer". I wonder! No-one saw where he went, I take it?

Kate For God's sake! Here we are, all suspecting each other of being scheming psychopaths ... I mean, the poor chap may simply have been taken short and gone to the loo!

Pause

Derek When you went back to your dressing-room, Kate ... Angela wasn't there, right?

Kate No.

Derek Well, isn't that a bit strange? She had a quick change too ... she should've been changing into her nightgown.

Kate So?

Derek Didn't you think it curious at the time ... that she wasn't there?

Kate No ... why should I? This is the first time we've run the play in costume. I didn't even know what she intended to wear ... let alone where she was going to do the change. Maybe in the wings, I don't know.

Martin She had already put on her nightgown!

Derek You mean she ...?

Martin Yes. ... That lengthens your odds a bit, I suppose, doesn't it?

Derek looks puzzled

She must have changed her costume during the scene drop ... that was your only opportunity!

Derek (*smiling*) Yes ... that's true!

Kate And Frank's too, come to that!

Pause

Derek Wait a minute ... wait a minute! Aren't we forgetting something? When Angela was off ... Frank sent Pam to look for her ... she was gone ... ten minutes! More ...! Plenty of time to kill Angela and fake the discovery of the body.

Pamela If you think I could have ...!

Martin Now hold on, Derek! In that case why did Angela miss her entrance ... if she wasn't killed till later?

Derek That question will have to remain unanswered ... for the moment! (*After a pause*) Well now ... where does that leave us? (*After a pause*) Looking at it purely in terms of opportunity ... I'd say Martin was the rank outsider, wouldn't you agree? He had no opportunity at all! As for myself and Frank ... a minute or so at the end of the scene change ...? I don't really think so! I suggest twenty-to-one would be fair odds for the two of us. ... Then we come to Kate ... five minutes more, wasn't it? You'll have to be three-to-one, I'm afraid Katy, dear! But the odds-on favourite ... in my book, anyway ... is our Pamela with ten minutes! Is THAT what you wanted to year, Pam? Does THAT put your mind at rest?

Pause

Martin Haven't you left somebody out?

Derek Who?

Martin Arthur Leadwood.

Pause. They all look at each other

Kate Why should Arthur Leadwood want to kill Angela?

Martin Why should any of US want to kill Angela? At the moment motive is not our strong suit, whichever way you look at it!

Kate Well, I don't buy that!

Derek Why not? Here we are accusing each other, and the most obvious candidate is our illustrious employer.

Kate But why?

Derek He must tie in somewhere!

Kate Why would he kill Angela with half a dozen witnesses around? If you want to murder someone . . . you . . . lure them to a remote spot, surely . . . on their own . . . with nobody around!

Derek We're not exactly witnesses . . . none of us saw him do it.

Martin Maybe not, but we ARE all here to testify to the fact that he brought us to this place. As soon as the police arrive, we'll tell them why we come to be here and "bingo!", Leadwood is arrested . . . case solved . . . he can't be that stupid.

Derek I'm not saying he IS that stupid. At the moment we've no proof he's been here at all.

Martin Unless . . . no!

Kate What?

Martin Nothing . . . nothing . . . I was just thinking aloud.

Derek Unless what, Martin?

Martin (*reluctantly*) Unless . . . well . . . he's lured us ALL to a remote spot, hasn't he . . .? On our own . . . nobody else around!

Pause

Kate You mean he wants to kill all six of us . . .?

Martin Now I didn't say that!

Kate . . . starting with Angela?

Pamela That's absurd!

Martin That was in no way intended as a serious suggestion . . . I was just thinking aloud!

Derek I'm not so sure. . . .

Kate Oh Derek, come on!

Derek Why did he want us to do this play . . . in his own theatre . . . in his own house . . . for just one performance?

Martin He wrote the play . . . he wanted to see it performed . . . that's natural enough! And what about all his friends in the audience? More witnesses?

Kate That's a point . . . the audience! They should all be here soon!

Derek How do we know there's going to be an audience? How do we know anyone's been invited here tonight? Perhaps . . . there's just an audience of one!

Pause

Martin Then why us?

Derek Exactly! Why us? Frank didn't cast us, did he? Leadwood specifically chose all six of us, right down to Pam as stage-manager. Why? If he's got it in for all of us . . . for whatever reason . . . and he wanted to get us all alone together, without arousing our suspicions . . . what could be more natural than to offer us all jobs doing the same play? HIS play!

Kate But what could he possibly have against US? None of us know him . . . or have ever heard of him before!

Pamela Frank knows him.

They all look at Pamela

Well doesn't he?

Kate Yes, of course he does. Frank must've met him!

Martin Or has he?

Pamela What do you mean?

Martin How do we know for sure? Frank never mentioned they'd met. The initial offer came by post, I know that. The script too.

Derek So if Frank hasn't met him either. . . .

Kate But he must have. . . .

Martin Now hold on, this isn't getting us anywhere. Let's wait for Frank to come back and we'll ask him. I'm sure he can vouch for Leadwood one hundred per cent!

Kate You've been reading too many detective stories, Derek.

Martin Too many plays, more like it!

Derek What do you mean by that?

Martin I don't mean anything, Derek. Why don't we wait for Frank to come back with the police and let them sort it out?

Derek What did you mean, "too many plays?"

Martin (*reluctantly*) Isn't it obvious? It's *The Domino Man*, isn't it? A group of people are lured, under pretext, to a remote Italian villa . . . they're all killed off one by one, all right? A group of actors are lured, under pretext, to a remote country house . . . they are all . . . whatever! It's the play! That's what put it into your mind. It's auto-suggestion, that's all!

Pause. Derek turns away in confusion. Pamela emits an involuntary gasp

Kate What is it, Pam?

Pamela I've just had a horrible thought!

Martin What?

Pamela In the play. Angela's character is the last to die.

Kate So?

Pamela So . . . how does she die . . .? In the play?

Pause

They all look at each other

Kate (*quietly*) She's strangled. . . .

Pause

Martin Coincidence!

Derek Is it? (*After a pause*) When we were offered this job . . . had anybody's agent heard of this Leadwood character before?

Kate No.

Pamela No.

Derek Mine neither . . . Martin?

Martin No . . . I don't think so . . . I didn't ask him.

Derek And if Frank was paid our money in advance . . . that would imply that Equity didn't know of him either. I mean it's a union rule, isn't it,

that if Equity haven't had previous dealings with an employer he has to
pay a deposit? Isn't that right?

Kate I . . . believe so, yes.

Derek So . . . it would appear that nobody in the business has ever heard of
Arthur Leadwood! Isn't that comforting?

Pause

Pamela Why do we have to sit here talking about it? Why can't we all just
leave?

Martin Frank will be back soon. I don't think the police would appreciate it
if we all suddenly fled the scene of the crime. (*To Pamela*) Would you like
some more brandy?

Pamela No.

Derek I would!

Martin hands him the flask. He drinks and puts the flask on the large table

Pause

Kate Where did you know Angela before, Martin?

Martin Er . . . I met her in Australia . . . I was working in Sydney for a while
. . . she was there for a month . . . on tour. We bumped into each other a
few times.

Kate Did you know her well?

Martin No . . . not really.

Kate You didn't . . . get together . . . as it were?

Derek A quickie affair, eh?

Martin Not in the least . . . she isn't . . . she wasn't like that.

Derek How do we know that's the truth?

Martin You'll just have to take my word for it, won't you?

Pause

Kate Did you know . . . her husband?

Martin I didn't know her that well . . . it was none of my business. Was she
married?

Kate She wore a wedding ring.

Derek Perhaps she was Mrs Arthur Leadwood!

Pamela Have you no respect for the dead? (*After a pause*) Don't you think
Frank's been gone long enough? Shouldn't one of us go and look for him?

Martin Maybe he can't find a telephone. It's a large house.

Derek Maybe . . . he's the murderer and he's made a run for it.

Kate Oh Derek, come on!

Derek Well why not? Or he might be out there in the house somewhere,
waiting for one of us to go and find him.

Martin The "two-minute murderer", you mean?

Derek It's possible!

Martin Oh yes . . . the possibilities are endless!

Derek On the other hand . . . if Leadwood is our man . . . then maybe
Frank's already dead.

Martin Now look ... we're all jumping to far too many conclusions. I say one of us should go and look for Frank and find a telephone.

Derek Then he or she can do a bunk as well ... as you say, the possibilities are endless!

Kate Well if you think I'm going down those corridors only to be leapt on by some seven foot suit of armour wielding a ball and chain, you've got another think coming. Count me out!

Pamela Why can't we all go?

Kate I am not budging from this spot until the police arrive! I think ... one of you "Knights Errant" should go and find Frank ... the other can stay here and protect us poor females. Off you go, Derek!

Derek Now wait a minute, wait a minute! I think this all boils down to who we can trust the most, don't you? I mean ... er ... who we can trust not to desert the sinking ship. As far as I'm concerned Leadwood is now the odds-on favourite, though Frank's odds have certainly shortened. As for me ... well I may have moved out a little in the betting ... but whichever way you look at it, Martin here is still the rank outsider. I think he should go. Somehow I think he ... WILL come back. What do you say?

Kate Sort it out between you ... I don't care!

Martin It's all right, I'll go. I don't mind.

Derek Spoken like a true hero! Why don't you go with him, Pam, if you're so keen?

Kate (*leaping to put her arm around Pamela*) You're not leaving me alone with HIM!

Pamela I don't know what to think. I'm scared.

Kate comforts her

I'll do ... whatever Kate wants. (*She grips Kate's hand*)

Martin OK. I'll be as quick as I can. (*He starts to go*)

Derek Here ... take this! (*He picks up the dagger and holds it out to Martin*)

Martin looks puzzled

It's real ... you might as well.

Martin looks to the girls, then back to Derek, hesitates, then takes the dagger and exits through the french windows

Derek takes the flask and crosses to the cocktail cabinet. He pours some brandy into a glass and drinks deeply. He has his back to the girls

Kate I've always wondered what that yellow streak was down your back, Derek.

Derek Right now I'm concerned only with my neck and its preservation. If that means being a coward, then so be it! (*He drinks*)

Pause

Pamela (*to Kate*) What do you think happened to poor Angela?

Kate I don't know ... I really do not know! And, at this moment in time, I don't want to know. All I want is for those boys in blue to come galloping in on their white chargers and take us away from all this.

Derek Perhaps Frank got through to the police and they said wait for them at the main entrance or something.

Kate I dearly hope so.

Derek And yet ... I don't know ... am I building this up into something that it isn't? I mean ... I keep coming back to this play, *The Domino Man*. ... A bunch of characters find themselves alone in this villa on one particular night. ... A bunch of actors find themselves alone in this house on this particular night. ... Then we find Angela strangled ... this same way she dies in the play, for God's sake! What does it mean? Is it coincidence? Or does it really mean something?

Kate It means you're going round in circles. If I were you, I'd drop the whole idea. Anyway, you're forgetting something ... in the play your death is faked and you re-appear at the end. ... YOU are the murderer, remember?

Derek (*smiling*) Don't think that hasn't occurred to me, Kate! That, of course, is where the parallel ends. ...

Kate Does it?

Derek Of course it does. I certainly didn't kill Angela ... and I've no intention of killing any of you.

Kate Lucky for you, I think this whole connection with the play is a load of hooey, anyway. I don't think you've got the guts to kill anyone.

Derek Thank you! Even so, the similarities up to that point are ... shall we say ... intriguing.

Pamela Nevertheless I'd feel happier if you stayed that side of the stage ... if you don't mind?

Derek As you wish. ... Brandy, anyone? (*He holds up the flask*)

Kate No, thank you.

Derek Or would you prefer some ... (*he picks up the "prop" Irish whiskey bottle*) hundred per cent proof burnt sugar water?

Kate That'll do, Derek!

Derek Oh yes, of course, it's laced with cyanide, isn't it?

Sound of a door banging loudly

They all react

Pamela What was that?

We hear footsteps coming towards them

Kate and Pamela jump up and retreat

> *Martin staggers through the french windows. He has blood on his face and is out of breath*

Pamela cries out

Martin It's all right ... it's all right. ... I'm OK!

Kate Martin, what happened?

Martin I got as far as the main staircase ... the light on the stairwell wasn't working. ... I started to walk down ... then I tripped and fell. ... I hit my head on the balustrade. There was a trip-wire across the top step ... and there at the bottom was Frank. ... He's dead. ...

Kate gasps

Pamela Oh my God, no!

Martin His neck is broken!

Derek End of scene three ... Franco's body is found on the patio. ... He has fallen from the balcony. ... HIS NECK IS BROKEN!

CURTAIN

SCENE 2

The same. A moment later

Kate Frank! Oh no it can't be ... it can't be true!

Martin I only wish it weren't, believe me!

Derek It has to be Leadwood. There's no other possible explanation. It has to be him.

Martin Now hold on, Derek. ...

Derek You think Frank will vouch for him now?

Pamela faints. Kate manages to catch her and Martin helps put her on the sofa. Kate sits next to her

Kate Some more brandy!

Martin pours some brandy into a glass and holds it for Pamela

Kate looks as though she too is going to faint

Derek You still say the connection with the play is a load of hooey? Well, it's getting just a little too close for comfort, if you ask me!

Kate God, it's so hot!

Martin Couldn't we do something about the lamps.

Kate We could put on the working lights, I suppose.

Martin OK.

Kate Martin ... would you ...? I don't think I could go out there.

Martin Sure. (*He hands the glass to Kate and starts to go*)

Kate The master switch is above the sound tape ... and to the right are three smaller switches ... they're the workers.

Martin exits R

Derek (*to Kate and Pamela*) Do you want to hear something funny? (*He shouts to Martin*) I said do you want to hear something funny?

The working lights come on. The stage lights go out as one

(*to himself*) I'm the only one here who hasn't been killed yet tonight. (*To Kate and Pamela*) Do you realize that?

Martin enters R, *dabbing the blood from his face with a tissue*

(*To all*) Do you realize I'm the only one of us here who hasn't been killed yet tonight? Don't you think that's funny? We start the dress rehearsal . . . and at the end of the first scene, Jennifer is suffocated with a pillow. (*He indicates Kate*) . . . Scene two and Brian here is poisoned with cyanide. (*He indicates Martin*) . . . and just as dear old David Lacey, the corrupt councillor, is about to be shot in the head, the play grinds to a halt. Then . . . our mysterious Arthur Leadwood takes over and decides to put his plot into reverse. . . . He starts at the end of the play and works backwards . . . only this time for real! Angela is strangled . . . FOR REAL . . . Franks gets his neck broken . . . FOR REAL . . . and any minute now yours truly is going to get his brains blown out . . . FOR REAL! Don't you find that hysterical?

Kate But your murder in the play is faked!

Derek I'm here to tell you, little lady, that if sometime in the next thirty minutes my grey matter is splattered all over this set, it sure as hell ain't gonna be no fake! (*He is now highly agitated*)

Kate Well then, what about Pam? She's not in the play. There are only five murders and there's six of us!

Martin SIX . . . murders . . .! Konakis' note, if you remember, is found beside the body of a dead fox. . . . Pamela . . . FOX!

Pamela But that's absurd . . . that's ridiculous!

Martin Of course it's ridiculous. This whole thing is ridiculous. Don't start looking for logic, Pam, because you won't find any.

Derek (*quietly*) Oh my God. . . .

Pamela I still say it could be one of you!

Derek Oh yes . . . and who do you have in mind? We were all here when Frank bought it, remember?

Pamela Except Martin!

Derek Oh sure. Martin is the only one of us who could have killed Frank. He is also the only one of us who could NOT have killed Angela. Where does that leave you? Two murderers? Somehow I don't think so!

Pamela Why not you, then?

Derek I was here, I tell you!

Pamela You could've set up that trip-wire at any time since we arrived. Even once the dress rehearsal had started . . . during the first scene between Martin and Kate.

Derek Oh wonderful!

Martin So could any of us . . .! We all had an opportunity to set up that wire . . . and cut the phone too, come to that.

Derek What phone? You found a phone?

Martin Yes, I found it all right . . . downstairs in the hallway . . . with the cord ripped out.

Derek The same as in the play . . . in the hallway with the cord ripped out!

Martin AND . . . the minibus has gone.

Kate What?

Martin The minibus . . . it's not in the driveway . . . it's gone!

Derek Well that settles it! If you think I'm waiting around here to be blown to kingdom come, you're very much mistaken. I'm getting out of here!

Martin (*grabbing hold of Derek*) Now hold it, Derek, hold it! These corridors are full of weapons . . . including ANTIQUE PISTOLS!

Derek (*moving backwards*) Well let's go out through the theatre, then.

Kate You can't. All the doors are bolted on the outside. I tried to go exploring before the rehearsal. There's no way out!

Martin Whichever way we go, we've got to stick together and be VERY careful. If Leadwood laid a trap for Frank . . . he could just as easily do the same for any of us. Now firstly . . .

Sudden Black-out

Martin Nobody move!

Pamela		Oh my God . . . what happened . . .? Kate . . .? Kate,
Kate	(*together*)	where are you? The lights . . . somebody get the lights.
Derek		. . . Over here, Pam! No, no . . . don't kill me. . . . Please . . . don't kill me!

Martin exits R

Pamela screams

Eventually all the stage lights come on but not the working lights

All are terrified, especially Derek who has retreated against the wall

Kate Martin . . .! Martin!

Martin (*off*) I'm here . . . all the lights have gone backstage.

Martin enters R

Somebody must've thrown the main switch . . . they've gone in the house too. Luckily the stage lights are on a different circuit.

Kate The black-out . . . at the end of scene two!

Martin Yes, I know . . . Pam . . .! Do we have a torch anywhere?

Pamela It's in the minibus. . . .

Martin Now, how do we get out of here?

Derek Whose great idea was it to turn off the stage lights?

Kate It was mine, if you must know.

Derek Why? WHY?

Kate It was hot . . .! No other reason.

Martin Stop it, both of you! Let's stop fighting each other, shall we?

Kate If only this were a bad dream . . . maybe it is . . . maybe Frank and Angela aren't really dead at all.

Pamela I found Angela! If you think I imagined that poor girl lying there . . . I shall never forget those eyes as long as I live! (*She sobs*)

Martin (*comforting her*) It's all right, Pam. . . . We know you didn't imagine it.

Kate Oh I'm sorry, Martin, I'm sorry. . . . I wasn't thinking.

Derek Well think now, damn you! He's out there somewhere. . . . I know he is!

Martin All right! So we accept that Leadwood is here . . . somewhere . . . in the building. But why is he doing this . . .? Why is he playing games with us?

Derek Games? I'm next on the list. . . . I'm about to be shot in the head . . . and you call it PLAYING GAMES!

Martin Come on, Derek, pull yourself together. That black-out comes at the end of scene two, remember? Not long AFTER you are supposedly shot. . . . Now if Leadwood is acting out his play in reverse, that means YOU haven't got much time . . . so try and think rationally! If we're all going to get out of this . . . and I mean *all* . . . then we've got to stick together!

Derek What can we do? What can we do? How do we stop him?

Martin If he DOES want to kill us all . . . why is he doing it this way? Why is he going through this elaborate performance?

Pamela He's a madman. He must be a sadist.

Derek He's probably watching us now . . . enjoying every minute of it.

Martin But why go to all this trouble? Why arrange for us all to come here, perform his play, let it proceed for a couple of scenes, then stop it and kill us one by one . . .? In the manner of the play! It's all too easy!

Derek Easy? My God!

Martin It's all too easy for us to discover that's what he's doing! Oh it took a while . . . we were a bit slow on the uptake. . . . We wasted too much time accusing each other. But eventually the penny dropped. . . . Now that two of us are dead . . . in the manner of the play . . . we KNOW what he's doing. . . . He's telling us . . . he's even laying extra clues for us; the black-out, the telephone. So we now know, at any given point, what is going to happen next.

Derek I know what's going to happen next and none of you seem to care a damn!

Kate So we know! How does that help us? It just makes it worse!

Martin We're missing something . . . we MUST be missing something. Why is he showing his hand? Why tell us his next move? Unless . . . maybe . . . there's something, somewhere . . . some way we can stop him.

Kate Why is he doing it in reverse?

Derek Whichever way he does it, I'm next, can't you see? For God's sake do something!

Martin If the play is now working backwards . . . then maybe there's something at the BEGINNING of the play that he doesn't want us to . . . hit upon . . . to discover . . . until it's too late.

Derek It's too late now, damn you!

Martin At the same time he's giving us the opportunity to find it if we can . . . he's playing with us . . .! He's teasing us. . . . What happens in the play before anyone is killed?

Kate Well . . . let me see . . . there's the drinks . . . the five bottles on the cocktail cabinet.

Martin Yes . . . but what could THEY mean? That doesn't lead us anywhere.

Kate There's the note . . . from Konakis.

Martin "Confess your sins and you will be saved. . . ."

Pamela That doesn't mean anything either. . . .

Martin Or does it . . .? I wonder . . . maybe that's the way we can put a stop to it! (*He begins to work it out in his mind*) In the play they find the note before anyone dies, right ...? So they are given the opportunity to save themselves ... if they confess how they betrayed Konakis ... then he'll spare them ... having first of all discovered who Konakis really is.

Kate I don't follow.

Martin None of them has ever met Konakis. All they know is ... he owns the villa ... and he's arranged for them all to be here. ...

Derek None of US has ever met Leadwood ... he owns this house ... he's arranged for all of US to be here. ...

Martin And if Leadwood is Konakis ... then he's also *The Domino Man* ... the man in disguise!

Derek So ... he's not Leadwood at all!

Martin Precisely! He's not Leadwood at all ... he's someone from OUR past ... that WE all know ... that WE betrayed at sometime or other. And by doing the play in reverse ... we don't get to that message outside the door ... until it's too late ... and we're all dead!

Derek If we can discover his real identity and confess what we did to HIM ... then he'll spare us!

Kate But in the play they NEVER find out who Konakis is!

Martin Then we'll just have to try that much harder than they did, won't we? Leadwood wants revenge! He'll kill us all if necessary ... but he'll be quite happy to watch us torturing ourselves trying to find out who he is. Hence this fantastic charade!

Derek Then who is he? WHO IS HE?

Martin We must think ... fast ... all of us. ...

Derek (*softly*) ... Everybody we've harmed ... however remotely ... in the past! My God, that's my line from the play!

Pamela But Derek's murder is faked! HE is the murderer!

Derek For God's sake, I swear I have nothing to do with this. Believe me ... for God's sake believe me ... I'm telling the truth!

Martin How does Konakis fit into the play? He's rich and he owns the villa. ... OK, so Leadwood is rich and he owns this house. ...

Kate And the theatre that goes with it. What if he IS something to do with "the business" after all?

Martin What about you two girls? An unhappy love affair, or something.

Kate Oh darling, too many to count!

Pamela (*distraught*) I ... I once had a car accident. The ... other driver was badly hurt. He was paralysed. But it wasn't my fault ... I swear it wasn't my fault!

Martin What was his name?

Pamela He came out of a side-turning ... suddenly ... I didn't even see him!

Martin His name, Pamela! What was his NAME?

Pamela Er ... er ... his name ...! Er ... Courtney, Courtney was his name ... I think ... yes, George Courtney.

Martin Doesn't mean anything to me. Anyone else?

Kate No.

Martin Derek?

Derek (*preoccupied with his own misery*) I can't think straight. I can't think straight!

Pause

Kate (*weakly*) I . . . I was engaged to be married once . . . a long time ago. . . . He was a struggling actor at the time . . . well . . . I'm afraid I jilted him at the last moment . . . the day before the ceremony, to be precise. He pestered me for months and months to go back to him . . . I just told him to get lost!

Martin Well . . .?

Kate I've regretted it ever since, of course. . . . (*She looks around the theatre*) . . . He's now a very rich man!

Martin Kate . . .!

Kate But it can't be him, it can't be. . . . He's devious, yes . . . and almost certainly a crook . . . but . . . THIS?

Martin His NAME, Kate . . .?

Kate Howard . . .! Howard de la Tour!

They all react. Derek is thunderstruck, but tries desperately not to show it

Pause

Martin Well . . . we all know OF him, of course . . . and . . . he fits the bill. . . .

Kate But did you know him personally . . . any of you . . . in the past?

Martin I knew him. . . .

Kate Pamela?

Pamela (*quietly*) Yes. . . .

Martin Derek?

Derek (*very frightened*) Well I . . . I've heard of him . . . of course. . . . Everybody knows de la Tour. But I've never met the man!

While Martin and Pamela tell their stories, they are acutely aware of a "Fourth Person" listening to them somewhere in the theatre. They are "confessing" to him as well as the others

Martin I knew him twenty-odd years ago . . . we were both straight out of drama school . . . we were in the same year! There was a whole load of us up for a part in a TV series. . . . A young boy . . . late teens . . . it was a year's work . . . a lot of money. Well . . . they got it down to a short list of two . . . me and Howard! It stayed that way for a fortnight . . . God! They were the longest two weeks of my life. I was young, ambitious and . . . I sent a letter to the director of the series. . . . It was supposedly from Howard's agent . . . saying that Howard had accepted another offer and was no longer available for the job. Well, I got the part . . . I don't know if the letter had anything to do with it, but from that day . . . Howard never spoke to me again! (*He looks around*) I always suspected he knew!

Pamela rises and crosses to the R

Derek Look, it can't be him, I tell you. I've never had any dealings with him . . . it MUST be somebody else!

Pamela (*turning to face them*) I was company manager on the first tour that
  Howard ever put on the road. I also did the bookkeeping. Business was
  bad ... not disastrous but ... poor. At the end of the eighth week, twenty-
  five thousand pounds went missing. Howard couldn't pay the cast ... the
  tour folded. As a result ... he lost another five thousand in various claims.
  (*She crosses to the large table*) I'd taken the money ... the two-and-a-half
  thousand! I'd falsified the accounts. Howard knew, all right ... he
  accused me to my face ... but he couldn't prove anything.... I was very
  clever. Needless to say, I've never worked for him since ... (*she looks
  around*) ... until NOW, that is! (*She looks down at her script on the table*)
Derek (*in agitation*) Are you all deaf, or something? Will you stop harping
  on about Howard de la Tour! It's not him, I tell you! It's somebody else!
Martin Derek, you must've made a mistake ... you must've known him
  somewhere! Think again!
Derek I tell you I've never met the bast ...! It's someone else! It HAS to be!

Pamela picks up her pen and begins to write

Kate (*preoccupied*) I wonder what Angela and Frank did to him.
Martin We shall never know.
Kate Angela and I were talking once during rehearsals ... I remember
  Howard came up in the conversation. She said, "I never want to hear that
  man's name again!" Now I know what she meant!
Derek Look, de la Tour disappeared, didn't he ...? Weeks ago! He's
  probably in South Africa or Australia by now. How can it possibly be
  him?
Martin They say his company was about to crash ... owing a lot of money.
Kate So Howard does "a Lord Lucan".... Typical!
Pamela If you still have any lingering doubts, Derek, take a look! (*She holds
  out her script*)

Derek ignores her but Martin takes it and studies what she has written

Kate What is it?
Pamela Arthur Leadwood and Howard de la Tour. ...
Martin One is an anagram of the other!

*Derek reacts to this and grabs the script from Martin. He sees what is written
there, then lets it fall*

Derek It isn't possible! It isn't possible!
Martin ... You must've known him. What happened between you?
Kate Come on, Derek ... if you didn't know him, your wife certainly did!
Derek No, no!
Kate Rebecca and I were at Salisbury together ... she confided in me ... she
  was having an affair with Howard!
Derek It isn't true, I tell you, it isn't true!
Kate Look, I'm sorry if you didn't know ... but this is no time for niceties.

Derek is beginning to sob. He sinks to his knees

Martin (*grabbing hold of Derek*) Listen to me, Derek! We know what
  Howard did to YOU.... What did you do to HIM? Tell us!

Derek Nothing! I did nothing!

Kate For pity's sake, Derek, tell us. It need go no further. . . .

Derek No! No!

Sound of a thunderclap

All the lights go out save for two pools of light where the actors are positioned

Derek emits a cry of terror

Lightning flashes outside the french windows. Thunder and lightning continue as the scene proceeds

Pamela Oh my God!

Kate It's the storm from the second scene!

Martin (*loudly, but carefully, as if explaining to a child*) Listen to me, Derek, listen to me! We are now back in the play. The storm has begun. There's lightning outside the windows!

Sound of thunder

Derek (*whimpering*) No, no!

Martin Listen to me, Derek, listen to me! This is where you are shot, remember? You must tell us what you did to Howard. Admit it . . . openly . . . now! Or else it will be too late! Howard will kill you!

Sound of thunder

   A figure, (Frank) now standing in the french windows, is silhouetted by the lightning. He wears a "Domino" hood and carries a gun

Pamela screams

Derek Stop him, please, stop him!

Martin Look, Derek, look! (*He turns Derek to face the figure*) Tell us what you did to him!

Sound of thunder

We hear Konakis' sinister voice on tape

Voice (*off*) Confess your sins and you will be saved!

Sound of loud thunderclap

Martin Confess, Derek, and he will stop . . . NOW!

More lightning

Derek No, no!

Martin Confess to him! Ask his forgiveness!

Sound of thunder

Derek No, Howard, no . . . I killed you . . . I killed you, Howard. . . .

Sound of thunder

Martin But he's here, Derek. HE'S HERE!

Derek (*to Martin, in utter desperation*) No, he can't be! He came to my house and I killed him! I hit him, again and again and again! I killed him, I tell you! I buried him in the garden! I buried him with my bare hands!

Sound of thunder

Martin lets Derek go. He sinks to the floor

Oh Rebecca, Rebecca ... I couldn't help myself!

The thunder dies away. The lightning stops but the lightning light stays on through the french windows

Derek lies in a heap

Martin stands slowly, crosses to the cocktail cabinet and takes out the gun from the drawer

The pools of light brighten a little

Martin turns to face Derek, pointing the gun at him

Kate and Pamela react audibly

Martin Don't worry. You're both quite safe.

Frank removes his "Domino" hood and steps forward

Kate Frank ...! What's happening?
Frank As you can see ... I'm very much alive.
Martin Frank's gun may not be real, Derek ... but I'm afraid this one is.
Kate How did that gun get there?
Martin I put it there ... during the first scene. I couldn't carry it around with me, but I wanted it close at hand ... I thought I might need it. Now ... I'm not so sure!
Kate Would somebody mind telling me what the hell is going on?
Martin I'm afraid that I ... am Arthur Leadwood! At least, I'm certainly responsible for everything that's happened here this evening. But I meant no harm to either of you ... it's Derek I wanted.
Pamela You mean ... you knew? You knew Derek had killed Howard?
Martin Oh yes, I knew! That is ... I was as certain as any man could be. But I couldn't prove it.
Kate So this whole thing ... was a trap? To make him confess?
Martin In a way, yes. You see ... a confession alone was not enough. We needed to know what he'd done with Howard's body. Without that ... we couldn't prove he'd done anything!
Frank You know ... there were times I never thought he'd crack, but. ...
Martin He did! Perhaps you ladies would like to sit down.

They sit

Frank I don't think we quite realized what effect all this was going to have ... on you ... or us, for that matter. I'm sorry if we frightened you.
Martin Kate ... Pam ... what can I say? I'm truly sorry. But there was no other way. If there had been, believe me, I would have tried it.

Kate But what's all this got to do with you? Either of you?

Martin Perhaps I should explain.

Pamela I think perhaps you should.

Martin My name ... as you have probably gathered ... is not Arthur
Leadwood. But it is Martin ... it's Martin de la Tour. Howard was my
brother! To begin at the beginning. ... I've been in Australia for the last
ten years, trying to eke out a living in the theatre. I came back to this
country about three months ago. Now Howard and I were never very
close but ... well ... he was my brother. So I contacted him and we
arranged to meet. ... We had a night out on the town ... we caught up on
each others gossip; the financial difficulties his company was in ... and
amongst other things, he told me about his affair with Rebecca Watson,
Derek's wife. She had by now left Derek and was living on her own.
Howard said Derek had found them together and threatened to kill him
...! He even laughed about it. Anyway, we arranged that he would come
to my place the following Sunday for lunch ... and we parted. That was
on the Monday. On Thursday, I was in town for an interview ... so I rang
Howard ... said "come for a drink". He said no, "he was off to meet the
cuckold at a place called Chelsea" ... his very words. Then he said, "See
you Sunday", and rang off. The cuckold I took to mean Derek ... "at a
place called Chelsea"? ... everyone knows Chelsea ... why refer to it as
"a place"? I didn't understand. And I didn't see or hear from Howard
again. The next day, nobody knew where he was. He'd vanished. Sunday
came and went ... but no Howard. So after a few days I went to look for
this Derek Watson ... he seemed to be the last person to see Howard
before he disappeared. I found out where he lived and went round there.
His house was a hundred yards away from a pub ... called *The
Chelsea*. So I put two and two together. Howard had been there the
night he disappeared ... the landlord remembered them both. They were
arguing, he said, quite violently ... and ... they left together! I grew
suspicious. I went to the police and told them what I knew ... they did
nothing ... they dismissed the whole idea. As far as they were concerned,
Howard had, as Kate so aptly put it, ... "done a Lord Lucan". But I
wasn't satisfied ... it didn't sound like Howard at all. Things were bad,
yes ... he told me so ... but not that bad ... not enough to warrant
running away. So I hired a private detective ... only for one day ... it's all
I could afford ... to follow Derek. He went nowhere in particular ... and
yet ... everywhere! He spent the whole day wandering around London ...
"a very frightened and nervous man", I was told. Occasionally he'd go
into a pub and order a large whisky ... "his hands shaking so much he
could hardly raise the glass to his lips". And whenever he saw a policeman
in the street ... "he'd dart down a side alley or hide in a doorway until
they'd gone". Hardly the behaviour of an innocent man. There seemed
only one possible explanation. Derek had ... "done away with him" ...
somehow. He'd carried out his threat. The question was ... how ... and
where?

*Derek stops sobbing and raises himsef to a kneeling position. His expression is
gaunt, exhausted, resigned, as if in a state of shock*

Martin Frank . . .! Would you mind? (*He hands his gun to Frank, who points it at Derek*)

Frank I assure you, Derek, this gun is . . . FOR REAL!

Martin I decided to lay a trap for him. . . . Angela and Frank agreed to help. Frank, by the way, is a true and trusted friend from way back.

Frank Howard also owed me a good deal of money. So you see . . . I had, what you might call . . . a vested interest in the outcome of tonight's performance.

Martin And so I hatched my elaborate plot, though at the time it didn't seem elaborate at all. It just . . . fell into place! This house does . . . did . . . belong to Howard. He told me about it the night we met . . . even gave me a set of keys. He said if ever Angela and I wanted to drive down and spend a weekend here. . . .

Angela enters R

we could make ourselves at home. Oh, . . . my wife . . . Angela!

Angela I phoned the police. They're on their way.

Pamela (*softly*) Angela! But . . .

Martin Howard was quite proud of his little theatre. "A rich man's toy", he called it. And the set was, indeed, already here. *The Domino Man* . . . I'd written myself . . . some years ago. Needless to say, it's never been performed . . . it's not that good a play . . . as you all pointed out on more than one occasion. But we decided to stage one performance . . . here! A professional production, of course! I rewrote it here and there to suit my purposes and the three of us would appear in it with Frank directing. The most important thing . . . naturally . . . was to get Derek to play the part of David Lacey. We decided not to approach him for six weeks . . . give him time to pull himself together so that he felt like working again. He was very reluctant at first but . . . in the end . . . Frank managed to persuade him. Then we needed to enlist two other people . . . one actress to play Jennifer . . . and a stage-manager. In order for the plan to work they had to be two people that Howard held an authentic grudge against from the past . . . and they had to be available to do the job. Well . . . there were quite a few candidates, I can tell you! But we chose you two. Once the three of you had agreed to do the play . . . we were ready to go!

Pamela But I saw Angela myself . . . those marks on her neck . . . and . . . her eyes!

Angela (*fingering her neck*) Just make-up, I'm afraid.

Frank And she is rather a good actress . . . when she tries!

Martin That was our first difficult moment . . . I thought you were never going to find her. You seemed to look everywhere except the stage-management room.

Frank In the end . . . I had to send you to make tea!

Kate But how did you know we'd connect all this with Howard?

Martin I didn't . . . not for certain. It had to be a gradual process, of course . . . I had to point you in the right direction and I had to prompt you a few times, I must admit. Whenever you went astray, I gently led you back on to the path I wanted you to take. But most of the time you did all the hard

work for me . . . especially Derek. And he DID prove to be the murderer.
Oh not the murderer YOU were looking for . . . but the murderer WE
were looking for!

Kate And the black-out . . . the storm . . . and Konakis' voice?

Martin Angela and Frank! That's why I had to put the play into reverse . . .
they had to be the first two to die so that I could enlist their services. Once
again, ladies, my apologies. I know it's not much consolation but . . . you
will get paid, of course. Howard's life was heavily insured and, as far as I
know, I'm the sole beneficiary. Not that there'll be much left after the
debts are paid, but with a bit of luck . . . we might manage a little . . . shall
we say . . . danger money!

Pause

Kate Well . . .! In the last two hours I've been shocked, frightened, terrified
and practically wet my knickers . . . but all in all . . . I've probably had one
of the most exciting evenings of my life!

Pamela How can you say that? I've been terrified out of my wits! They used
us! They used both of us . . . they had no right!

Kate Oh come on, Pam. You're not exactly a saint yourself, you know!
Howard may have been a charlatan, but you embezzled him out of two
and a half thousand, remember? You start making complaints to the
police and that just might creep into the conversation . . . might it not,
Martin?

Martin I see no reason why anybody should ever know about that. And if
nobody knows . . . they can't ask you to pay it back . . . can they?

Kate There you are, Pam! Come along old girl! (*She pulls Pamela up*) If I
know Howard, he's got a well-stocked bar in this house somewhere, I'm
going to get you blind drunk!

*Derek takes a flying leap towards Frank and grabs one of the guns, both of
which are now positioned in Frank's belt. He then stands C stage by the french
windows and points the gun at the others*

Pamela, Kate and Angela are stage R

*Frank and Martin are stage L. The three men are virtually in a straight line,
with Frank in the middle*

Derek Not so fast! Nobody move!

They all freeze

If anyone's going to get blind drunk, it's going to be me . . . but I'll be a
long, long way from here when I do! Oh, Martin . . . you're a very clever
man . . . I'll give you that. I didn't mean to kill Howard . . . it just . . . it just
sort of happened. But that doesn't mean I'd hesitate to kill anyone of
you . . .

*Kate takes a step towards Derek and he quickly turns and points the gun
straight at her*

I mean it, Kate . . . I've nothing to lose now!

Martin (*quickly taking the other gun from Frank's belt and pointing it at Derek*) Hold it right there, Derek. You so much as blink and I'll shoot.

Derek (*looking horrified, then smiling nervously*) You fire at me ... and I'll fire at your wife. (*He moves the gun in Angela's direction*)

Martin And vice versa ... but fortunately ... for somebody ... only one of these guns has real bullets ... the other ... is full of blanks. The question is ... which is which? So why don't you drop that gun and save us all a lot of trouble.

Derek (*looking alarmed*) You wouldn't ...?

Martin (*cocking the gun*) Are you prepared to take the risk?

Derek smiles uneasily and after a pause allows the gun to swivel on his forefinger

Sound of approaching police siren

Derek OK ... you win! (*He tosses the gun carefully on to the sofa*)

Martin (*indicating Derek's gun*) Kate, would you mind?

Derek makes a dash for the french windows and disappears off R

Martin Derek!

Martin follows to the french windows and points the gun after Derek

Martin (*off*) DEREK!

The siren stops

Martin enters

Don't worry, he won't get far.

Frank goes after Derek through the french windows and off R

Kate Why didn't you shoot?

Martin What with? Blank cartridges?

Pamela You mean ... he had the gun with the real bullets?

Martin What I mean is ... neither of us had a gun with real bullets. They were both filled with blanks.

Kate I read you totally wrong, Martin. (*She crosses to the cocktail cabinet*) I never thought you had it in you. (*She picks up the flask and pours some brandy into a glass*) Suddenly, I have an overwhelming desire for some of Pamela's coffee. You're a lucky girl, Angela. Here's to you ... Mr Domino Man!

CURTAIN

FURNITURE AND PROPERTY LIST

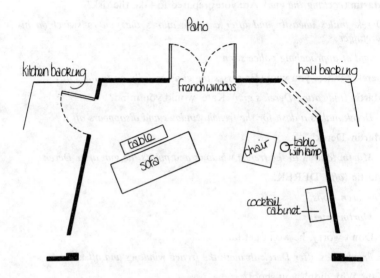

ACT I

SCENE 1

On stage: Sofa

Armchair

Large table. *On it:* magazines

Cocktail cabinet. *In it:* five bottles ... apple juice, Perrier water, Dubonnet, Irish Whiskey and Bourbon, glasses

Side table. *On it:* table lamp

Off stage: Two suitcases **(Brian)**

Ice **(Brian)**

Piece of paper and blood-stained dagger **(David)**

Personal: **Jennifer:** handbag containing a compact, cigarettes, lighter

Brian: gun in pocket

David: key, spectacles

Franco: slip of paper in pocket

SCENE 2

Set: Rug over **Brian**
             Jacket **(Brian's)** draped over the back of the sofa
             French windows closed
             Note on table

Off stage: Thermos flask **(Kate)**

Personal: **David:** dressing-gown
             Franco: watch, sheaves of paper in pocket, pen
             Pamela: hair tied back, spectacles, script of the play, newspaper with
                crossword, pen
             Kate: dressing-gown, tissues in pocket

ACT II

SCENE 1

Re-set: Thermos flask and Irish whiskey bottle on the cocktail cabinet

SCENE 2

Re-set: **Pamela**'s script on the table with a pen

Personal: **Martin:** tissue with blood on it
             Frank: "domino" hood, gun

LIGHTING PLOT

Practical fittings required: table lamp

Interior. A lounge. The same scene throughout

ACT I

To open: Subdued interior lighting with the remains of daylight showing through the french windows

| Cue 1 | **Jennifer** switches on the light | (Page 1) |
| | *Lights up* | |

| Cue 2 | **Brian** switches on table lamp | (Page 2) |
| | *Snap on lamp and covering spot* | |

| Cue 3 | **Brian** places the gun in the drawer | (Page 2) |
| | *The lights flicker, dim and come up* | |

| Cue 4 | **Jennifer:** "Perhaps he can explain what the hell is going on!" | (Page 6) |
| | *The lights flicker, dim and come up* | |

| Cue 5 | **Franco:** "It deadens the pain . . . does it not?" | (Page 12) |
| | *Black-out* | |

| Cue 6 | As Scene 2 opens | (Page 12) |
| | *Stage in darkness apart from a spill of light from the hall* | |

| Cue 7 | **David** switches on the kitchen light | (Page 12) |
| | *Lights up in kitchen* | |

| Cue 8 | **Franco** switches on the table lamp | (Page 12) |
| | *Snap on lamp and covering spot* | |

| Cue 9 | **Frank:** "At the moment the play is deader than you are." | (Page 14) |
| | *Lights up* | |

| Cue 10 | **Pamela** bursts into loud sobbing | (Page 25) |
| | *Black-out* | |

ACT II

To open: Full general lighting

| Cue 11 | **Derek:** "HIS NECK IS BROKEN!" | (Page 37) |
| | *Black-out* | |

| Cue 12 | As Scene 2 opens | (Page 37) |
| | *Full general lighting* | |

| Cue 13 | **Derek:** "I said do you want to hear something funny?" | (Page 37) |
| | *Working lights up. Stage lights out* | |

Cue 14 **Martin:** "Now firstly . . ." (Page 39)
Black-out

Cue 15 **Pamela** screams (Page 39)
Stage lights up, but not the working lights

Cue 16 Sound of thunderclap (Page 44)
Lights out save for two pools of light where the actors are standing, then a flash of lightning outside the french windows. The lightning to continue intermittently

Cue 17 A figure stands in the french windows (Page 44)
Flash of lighting

Cue 18 **Martin:** ". . . and he will stop . . . NOW!" (Page 44)
Flash of lightning

Cue 19 **Derek:** ". . . I couldn't help myself!" (Page 45)
The flashes of lightning stop but the lightning light stays on through the french windows

Cue 20 **Martin** takes the gun from the drawer (Page 45)
The pools of light brighten a little

Cue 21 **Kate:** "Here's to you . . . Mr Domino Man!" (Page 49)
Black-out

EFFECTS PLOT

ACT I

Cue 1 As the CURTAIN rises   (Page 1)
Sound of a car departing

Cue 2 **David:** "Someone must have left the lights on . . ."   (Page 4)
Sound of a key in the front door and the door opening

Cue 3 **Brian:** ". . . it's not important."   (Page 7)
Sound of front door bell

Cue 4 **Frank:** ". . . with any luck they won't flicker again."   (Page 24)
Sound of a door closing

ACT II

Cue 5 **Derek:** ". . . it's laced with cyanide, isn't it?"   (Page 36)
Sound of a door banging loudly

Cue 6 **Derek:** "No! No!"   (Page 44)
Sound of a thunder clap. Thunder and lighting continue intermittently

Cue 7 **Martin:** "There's lightning outside the windows!"   (Page 44)
Sound of thunder

Cue 8 **Martin:** "Howard will kill you!"   (Page 44)
Sound of thunder

Cue 9 **Martin:** "Tell us what you did to him!"   (Page 44)
Sound of thunder, then the taped voice and then another thunderclap

Cue 10 **Martin:** "Ask his forgiveness!"   (Page 44)
Sound of thunder

Cue 11 **Derek:** ". . . I killed you, Howard . . ."   (Page 44)
Sound of thunder

Cue 12 **Derek:** "I buried him with my bare hands!"   (Page 45)
Sound of thunder

Cue 13 **Derek:** ". . . I couldn't help myself!"   (Page 45)
The thunder dies away

Cue 14 **Derek** allows the gun to swivel on his forefinger   (Page 49)
Sound of approaching police siren

Cue 15 **Martin:** "DEREK!"   (Page 49)
The siren stops

MADE AND PRINTED IN GREAT BRITAIN BY
LATIMER TREND & COMPANY LTD PLYMOUTH

MADE IN ENGLAND